# Student Study G

## to accompany

# Exceptional Lives
## Special Education in Today's Schools

## Fifth Edition

**Ann Turnbull, Rud Turnbull, and Michael Wehmeyer**
*University of Kansas*

Prepared by
**Janna Siegel Robertson**
*University of Memphis*

PEARSON
Merrill
Prentice Hall

**Upper Saddle River, New Jersey**
**Columbus, Ohio**

**Vice President and Executive Publisher:** Jeffery W. Johnston
**Senior Editor:** Allyson P. Sharp
**Development Editor:** Linda K. Kauffman
**Editorial Assistant:** Kathleen S. Burk
**Production Editor:** Sheryl Glicker Langner
**Design Coordinator:** Diane C. Lorenzo
**Cover Design:** Ali Mohrman
**Production Manager:** Laura Messerly
**Director of Marketing:** David Gesell
**Marketing Manager:** Autumn Purdy
**Marketing Coordinator:** Brian Mounts

**Copyright © 2007, 2004, 2002, 1999, 1995 by Pearson Education, Inc., Upper Saddle River, New Jersey 07458.**
Pearson Prentice Hall. All rights reserved. Printed in the United States of America. This publication is protected by Copyright and permission should be obtained from the publisher prior to any prohibited reproduction, storage in a retrieval system, or transmission in any form or by any means, electronic, mechanical, photocopying, recording, or likewise. For information regarding permission(s), write to: Rights and Permissions Department.

**Pearson Prentice Hall™** is a trademark of Pearson Education, Inc.
**Pearson®** is a registered trademark of Pearson plc
**Prentice Hall®** is a registered trademark of Pearson Education, Inc.
**Merrill®** is a registered trademark of Pearson Education, Inc.

Pearson Education Ltd.
Pearson Education Singapore Pte. Ltd.
Pearson Education Canada, Ltd.
Pearson Education–Japan

Pearson Education Australia Pty. Limited
Pearson Education North Asia Ltd.
Pearson Educación de Mexico, S.A. de C.V.
Pearson Education Malaysia Pte. Ltd.

10 9 8 7 6 5 4 3 2 1
ISBN: 0-13-174084-9

# Introduction to Your Study Guide

## How Do I Use My Study Guide?

This study guide is designed to assist you when you use your textbook, *Exceptional Children: Special Education in Today's Schools,* Fifth Edition. Your professor has selected this book for its extensive coverage of content in the field of special education, for its exceptional emphasis on building partnerships with parents, for its focus on inclusion, and for its philosophy of providing the best education for students with disabilities using universal design and the general curriculum whenever possible. You will benefit from the use of this study guide because it will assist you in taking notes in class, involve you in activities to help you understand concepts, and help you study for assessments by using the practice quizzes.

## Objectives: Guiding Your Chapter Reading

Every chapter in the study guide begins with objectives that should guide your reading of the chapters in the book. You should read these objectives before you read the chapter and also when you finish reading the chapter. The objectives are also a good way to check your understanding of the content in the chapter. Can you do what the objectives ask you to do? Could you write a response to an essay question based on the objectives? After you finish the each chapter of the text and study guide, go back to the Objectives section in your study guide and check your learning.

## Standards Matrices: Relating Content to Professional Standards

The field of special education is guided by the professional standards of the Council for Exceptional Children (CEC) and PRAXIS™ standards, developed to help you with your professional certification tests. Each chapter of your study guide presents a matrix (table) of how these standards align with the content of the chapter. You can refer to the standards in the matrix to see what content is covered and how it relates to the standards, and you can also refer to the complete list of standards that appear in the Appendix at the back of your textbook. It is good practice to learn to associate the content of special education with these specific standards—to see the standards in action will help you as you move into your own classroom and use the standards to guide your professional decisions and teaching. Also, before you can teach, you will need to pass specific tests that are based on these standards…it's good to start learning those standards and how they apply to your field of study.

## Checking for Understanding: Key Terms

One of the best ways to check your understanding of the content in the chapters is to write down the definitions of key terms. Each chapter of the study guide includes a table of the key terms, with a place for you to write the definition, and a column for you to check that you have found the definition in the chapter and understand how the term is used. Though this may seem a simple task, it is actually a very good way to familiarize yourself with the important concepts in the chapter. Once you understand these concepts, you will have a good foundation for understanding the chapter contents.

## Chapter Outline: Taking Chapter Notes

Another great feature of the study guide is the chapter outline. ***This is the best way for you to take notes in class or to take notes as you read the chapter.*** You can tear out the chapter outline, take it to class, and take notes directly on the outline. This way, you don't have to waste time writing down everything from the PowerPoint slides or transparencies that your professor uses. Even if your professor doesn't use these tools, the outline can still be used to take notes—you can highlight, underline, and add your own notes as your professor leads the class or as you join in class discussions. This is also a good place to make notes about anything you didn't understand in the chapter. Your notes will remind you to ask your professor to clarify any information or concepts for you.

## Activities: Applying Your Learning

Each chapter in the study guide also includes some activities for you to use to help you apply your learning. The helpful thing about these activities is that they allow you to use the chapter content in a meaningful way. For instance, to give you an idea of the enormous amount of thought and information you need to adequately prepare an Individualized Education Program (IEP) for a student, you are asked to prepare one for yourself. You will also use different types of activities to tap into your own learning preferences. The activities might ask you to use a drawing, a song, or a dance to communicate and show mastery of concepts from the chapters. Another important thing to know is that these activities are also included in the Instructor's Manual, so your professor may ask you to complete some of these for homework. You will definitely have an advantage if you have already had a chance to think about these activities and apply your learning.

## Practice Quizzes: Assessing Your Knowledge

To give you an opportunity to check how well you learned the content in the chapters, there is a practice quiz for each chapter. You can check your answers to determine how successfully you have learned some of the information in the chapters. (The answers are provided for you at the end of your study guide.) Similar questions are also included in the test bank file that your instructor may use to make assessments for the class. Therefore, taking the practice quiz not only assures you that you have mastered chapter concepts; it could also assist in preparation for exams your instructor provides.

If you use this study guide to supplement your textbook and learning in this class, you should have a very successful experience and be rewarded by learning a great deal about this very important field. Hopefully you will take this knowledge with you as you move into your own classroom and become one of the new leaders in the field of special education.

# Table of Contents

# Chapter 1: Overview of Today's Special Education

## Objectives: Guiding Your Chapter Reading

The content in this chapter is presented to help you achieve the following objectives. Once you complete your study of the chapter, see if you can do what the objectives describe. If not, you may need to do some more reviewing of the chapter and your class notes.

- Describe the characteristics of special education
- Identify the disability categories
- Describe various stakeholders in special education
- Identify the basic components of IDEA
- Summarize laws that impact the lives of individuals with disabilities

## Standards Matrices: Relating Content to Professional Standards

The matrices, or charts, below help you see how the professional standards from the Council for Exceptional Children (CEC) and PRAXIS™ apply to the content in this chapter. In addition, you can refer to the margin notes throughout the chapter and the activities at the end of each chapter to make sure you understand how these standards apply to the content in the field of special education. These standards are important for you to know, because they provide the basis for the professional teacher certification examinations and content covered in these exams.

| CEC Standards | Topic |
|---|---|
| 1 | <ul><li>IDEA</li><li>Disproportionate representation</li><li>Zero reject</li><li>Expulsion and discipline</li><li>Procedural due process</li><li>Long-term results of special education</li><li>Socioeconomic characteristics</li><li>Family educational level</li><li>Racial and ethnic trends</li><li>Appropriate education</li></ul> |
| 2 | <ul><li>Case study</li><li>Long-term results of special education</li></ul> |
| 3 | <ul><li>Instructional needs of students with disabilities</li><li>Who are the students with disabilities?</li><li>Long-term results of special education</li><li>Family educational level</li><li>Racial and ethnic trends</li><li>Appropriate education</li></ul> |
| 4 | <ul><li>Who are students with disabilities?</li><li>Instructional needs of students with disabilities</li></ul> |
| 5 | <ul><li>Who are students with disabilities?</li><li>Instructional needs of students with disabilities</li><li>Expulsion and discipline</li><li>Parent-student participation</li></ul> |
| 6 | <ul><li>Parent-student participation</li></ul> |
| 7 | <ul><li>Who are students with disabilities?</li><li>Instructional needs of students with disabilities</li></ul> |

| 8 | • Who are students with disabilities? |
|---|---|
|   | • Instructional needs of students with disabilities |
|   | • Nondiscriminatory evaluation |
|   | • Appropriate education |
| 9 | • Disproportionate representation |
|   | • Special education personnel |
|   | • Zero reject |
|   | • Expulsion and discipline |
|   | • Overlapping services to support students with disabilities |
|   | • Procedural due process |
|   | • Long-term results of special education |
|   | • Racial and ethnic trends |
|   | • Appropriate education |
| 10 | • Special education personnel |
|   | • Parent-student participation |
|   | • Overlapping services to support students |

| PRAXIS™ Standards | Topic |
|---|---|
| 1 | • Who are students with disabilities? |
|   | • Instructional needs of students with disabilities |
|   | • Disproportionate representation |
| 2 | • Discrimination |
|   | • Judicial decisions |
|   | • Individuals with Disabilities Education Act |
|   | • Principles of IDEA |
|   | • Rehabilitation services |
|   | • Section 504 and the ADA |
| 3 | • Special education personnel |
|   | • Least restrictive environment |
|   | • Free appropriate public education |

## Checking for Understanding: Key Terms

To check that you understand the basic terms and vocabulary in the chapter, use the space provided to write the definitions or descriptions in your own words. Then, check the chapter to see how accurate your definition is, making sure you understand the context, or situation, in which the word is used. Reviewing these terms will help you better understand the concepts that support the content in this chapter.

| Term | Definition/Description | (✓) |
|---|---|---|
| alternative teacher certification | | |
| appropriate education | | |

| | | |
|---|---|---|
| zero reject | | |
| no cessation | | |
| manifestation determination | | |
| nondiscriminatory evaluation | | |
| screening prereferral | | |
| referral | | |
| Individualized Education Program (IEP) | | |
| Individualized Family Plan (IFSP) | | |
| least restrictive environment (LRE) | | |
| procedural due process | | |

| Additional Terms | | |
|---|---|---|
| special education | | |
| disabilities | | |
| person-first language | | |
| labeling | | |
| **Laws** | | |
| Rehabilitation Act | | |
| Technology-Related Assistance to Individuals with Disabilities Act (Tech Act) | | |
| Section 504 | | |
| Americans with Disabilities Act (ADA) | | |
| Individuals with Disabilities Education Act (IDEA) | | |
| No Child Left Behind (NCLB) | | |

## Chapter Outline: Taking Chapter Notes

The following outline is taken from the PowerPoint slides or overheads that your professor uses in class for this chapter. In the slides, there are several embedded links to more information for this chapter. Please go to the Companion Website at: http://www.prenhall.com/turnbull to access them easily.

If you take your Study Guide to class, you can use this outline for taking notes on the chapter or for review. It will also allow you to listen to lectures and participate in class discussions without having to copy down all the PowerPoint information.

The notes below are set up for recording information from the chapter in a particular way—an adapted Cornell method of taking notes. In this adapted Cornell method, you underline, or highlight, information presented to you. In addition to highlighting, you can write information or explanations on the left-hand side of the table. Soon after the class presentation or reading the chapter, rewrite the notes from the left-hand side in your own words, using key terms and phrases. To study for quizzes or exams, you can cover up the left hand side and use the right-hand side of the table to cue yourself about the information.

You also may just jot notes on the right-hand side to help you. Since this outline reduces the chapter for you, it will be a useful study aid. The summary at the end of the chapter is another useful resource to use for review.

| Chapter 1:<br>Overview of Today's Special Education | NOTES |
|---|---|
| [Slide 1-1] Chapter 1 Objectives: At the end of this chapter, you should be able to:<br>• Describe the characteristics of special education<br>• Identify the disability categories<br>• Describe various stakeholders in special education<br>• Identify the basic components of IDEA<br>• Summarize laws that impact the lives of individuals with disabilities | |
| [Slide 1-2] Who Is Thomas Ellenson?<br>• Thomas is a seven-year-old boy with cerebral palsy<br>• He and his family were featured in a story in the *New York Times Sunday Magazine*<br>• Thomas's dad, Richard, worked to create an advertising campaign for United Cerebral Palsy of New York City<br>• Richard and Thomas's mom, Lois, worked with the mayor of NYC to create a new inclusive education program in the city's school system | |
| [Slide 1-3] Values to Guide Teaching (See Figure 1–1)<br>• Envisioning Great Expectations<br>• Enhancing Positive Contributions<br>• Building on Strengths<br>• Becoming Self-Determined<br>• Expanding Relationships<br>• Ensuring Full Citizenship | |

| | |
|---|---|
| [Slide 1-4] Profile of Special Education<br>• Slightly over 6 million students<br>• Almost 272,454 infants and toddlers<br>• Almost 680,142 preschool children<br>• About 9% of school's enrolled population<br>• Increasing at a faster rate than non-disabled population | |
| [Slide 1-5] Profile of Special Education<br>• More boys than girls—especially in learning disabilities and emotional disturbance<br>• Why?<br>  • Physiological/maturational differences<br>  • Education bias<br>  • Assessment bias | |
| [Slide 1-6] Categories of Disabilities (See Figure 1–2) | |
| [Slide 1-7] Labeling<br>• Allows students with disabilities to receive services<br>• Labels may be stigmatizing or result in discrimination<br>• View children by their abilities not disabilities<br>• Use person-first language<br>• Guidelines for reporting and writing about people with disabilities | |
| [Slide 1-8] Who Works with Individuals with Special Needs?<br>• Special education is a high demand occupation<br>• Districts often have unfilled teaching positions<br>• Many different professionals work with students with disabilities | |
| [Slide 1-9] Two Types of Discrimination<br>• Previous discrimination:<br>  • Exclusion<br>  • Ineffective or inappropriate education<br>• Students were often misdiagnosed<br>• Consequences of *Brown v. Board of Education* (1954) | |

| | |
|---|---|
| [Slide 1-10] Court Cases<br><br>•*Mills v. Washington, DC, Board of Education* and *Pennsylvania Association for Retarded Citizens [PARC] v. Commonwealth of Pennsylvania*<br>    The courts ordered school districts to:<br>    — Provide a free, appropriate public education to all students with disabilities<br>    — Educate students with disabilities in the same schools and basically same programs as students without disabilities<br>    — Put into place procedural safeguards so that students can challenge schools that do not live up to the court's orders.<br>•These decisions led to families advocating for a federal law to guarantee rights | |
| [Slide 1-11] Introduction to IDEA<br>• IDEA (originally called Education of All Handicapped Students Act or PL 94-142) was first enacted in 1975<br>• Original intent: open schools to all students with disabilities and ensure they had a chance to benefit from special education<br>• Current focus: meet student goals and outcomes | |
| [Slide 1-12] Special Education and Students' Eligibility<br>• Eligibility is based on need<br>• Special education services are provided wherever there are students with disabilities<br>    ▪ Classrooms<br>    ▪ Students' homes<br>    ▪ Hospitals and institutions<br>    ▪ Other settings | |

| | |
|---|---|
| [Slide 1-13] Related Services (See Figure 1–3)<br>• Audiology<br>• Counseling services<br>• Early identification<br>• Family training, counseling, and home visits<br>• Health services<br>• Medical services<br>• Nursing services<br>• Nutrition services<br>• Occupational therapy<br>• Orientation and mobility services<br>• Parent counseling and training<br>• Physical therapy<br>• Psychological services<br>• Recreation and therapeutic recreation<br>• Rehabilitative counseling services<br>• School health services<br>• Service coordination services<br>• Social work services in schools<br>• Speech pathology and speech-language pathology<br>• Transportation and related costs<br>• Assistive technology and services | |
| [Slide 1-14] Students' Eligibility<br>•Eligibility : Two-part standard.<br><br>     •Categorical<br><br>     •The student must have a disability<br><br>     •Functional<br><br>     •The student must need specially designed services<br>•IDEA provides services from birth to age 21 (historically was from ages 6 to 18)<br>•IDEA has two sections:<br><br>     • Part B serves children ages 3 to 21<br><br>     • Part C serves students ages birth to 2 | |
| [Slide 1-15] Students' Eligibility<br>•Part B<br><br>     •12 disability categories under which students may be served.<br>•Part C benefits children under age 3 who:<br><br>     •Need early intervention services because of developmental delays.<br><br>     •Have a diagnosed physical or mental condition that has a high probability of resulting in a developmental delay.<br>States have the option of serving at-risk children. | |

| | |
|---|---|
| [Slide 1-16] IDEA Disability Categories<br>• Specific learning disabilities<br>• Emotional disturbance<br>• Mental retardation<br>• Multiple disabilities<br>• Deaf-blindness<br>• Autism<br>• Other health impairments<br>• Orthopedic impairments<br>• Traumatic brain injury<br>• Speech or language impairments<br>• Hearing impairments<br>• Visual impairments | |
| [Slide 1-17] Individuals with Disabilities Education Act:<br>Six Principles<br>• Zero reject<br>• Nondiscriminatory evaluation<br>• Appropriate education<br>• Least restrictive environment<br>• Procedural due process<br>• Parental and student participation | |
| [Slide 1-18] Zero Reject<br><br>•Prohibits schools from excluding any student with a disability from receiving a free, appropriate public education<br><br>•Applies to<br>      o    Educability<br>      o    Expulsion and discipline<br><br>•"no-cessation," "ten-day," "change of placement," "manifestation determination," "SBA/BIP," "stay-put," and "45-day" rules | |
| [Slide 1-19] Nondiscriminatory Evaluation: Two Purposes<br><br>•Does the student have a disability?<br><br>•What kind of special education and related services does the student require?<br><br>•Assessment requirements<br>    •Screening<br>    •Prereferral<br>    •Referral<br>    •Nondiscriminatory evaluation | |
| [Slide 1-20] Nondiscriminatory Evaluation: A funneling process (Figure 1–6) | |

| | |
|---|---|
| [Slide 1-21] Appropriate Education: IEP/IFSPs<br>• Individualized education for each student with a disability<br>• Developed collaboratively by the same people involved in the evaluation<br>• Outcome oriented (include goals/objectives)<br>• Provide the foundations for the student's appropriate education | |
| [Slide 1-22] IEPs and IFSPs<br>IEPs<br><br>•Document for students 3–21<br><br>•Need to be in effect at the beginning of the school year<br><br>•Reviewed and revised at least once a year<br>IFSPs<br><br>•Document for children ages 0–2<br><br>•Describes the services both the child and family will receive<br><br>•Should be developed within 45 days of referral and reviewed at 6-month intervals and every year thereafter | |
| [Slide 1-23] IEP Team and IEP Components<br>IEP Team<br>•Parents<br>•General educator<br>•Special educator<br>•School system representative<br>•Evaluation interpreter<br>•Others<br>•Student<br>IEP components<br>•Student's present level of performance<br>•Measurable annual goals and short-term objectives<br>•Special education and related services<br>•Explanation of the extent of time not in general setting<br>•Assessment participation and/or accommodations<br>•Transition plan | |

| | |
|---|---|
| **[Slide 1-24] IEP/IFSP Conferences**<br>1. Prepare in advance<br>2. Connect and get started<br>3. Review formal evaluation and current levels of performance<br>4. Share resources, priorities, and concerns<br>5. Share visions and great expectations<br>6. Consider interaction of proposed student goals, placements, and services<br>7. Translate student priorities into written goals<br>8. Determine placement, supplementary aids and related services<br>9. Address assessment modifications<br>10. Conclude the conference | |
| **[Slide 1-25] Least Restrictive Environment**<br>• Education with students who do not have disabilities<br>• For early childhood, IDEA favors the "natural environment"<br>• The rule: a presumption of inclusion<br>• Access to the general education curriculum<br>• Setting aside the presumption<br>• The continuum of services<br>• Extracurricular and nonacademic inclusion | |
| **[Slide 1-26] Procedural Due Process**<br>Makes schools and parents accountable to each other<br>•Mediation<br>    •The first step available<br>    •Not required by IDEA but strongly encouraged<br>•Due process hearing<br>    •An administrative, quasi-judicial hearing similar to a mini-trial<br>    •Conducted before a person who will make a qualified, objective decision<br>    •Parents and schools are entitled to have lawyers present<br>    •Required by IDEA to be an available process | |
| **[Slide 1-27] Parent Rights**<br>• Parents are members of teams<br>• Parents receive notification before schools do anything about their child's education<br>• Parents have access to school records concerning student<br>• At age of majority IDEA rights transfer to the student | |

| | |
|---|---|
| [Slide 1-28] Relationship among 6 principles (See Figure 1–8) | |
| [Slide 1-29] Federal Funding of the Individuals with Disabilities Education Act<br>• Congress grants federal money to state and local educational agencies<br>• The federal money is insufficient to provide all services<br>• States and local school districts must provide their own funds<br>• Special education services are expensive | |
| [Slide 1-30] Six Principles of No Child Left Behind<br>•Accountability for results<br>•School safety<br>•Parental choice<br>•Teacher quality<br>•Scientifically-based methods of teaching<br>•Local flexibility<br>Also<br>•Complements IDEA<br>•For more information see No Child Left Behind (NCLB)-2002 | |
| [Slide 1-31] Other Federal Laws: Entitlements and Antidiscrimination Rehabilitation Act<br>• Allows people to seek vocational rehabilitation services so they may work<br>• Provides services such as supported employment programs and job coaches<br>• Tech Act<br>• Allows states to create statewide systems for delivering assistive technology devices and support to people with disabilities | |
| [Slide 1-32] Other Federal Laws: Entitlements and Antidiscrimination Section 504<br>• Applies to any program or activity receiving federal funds<br>• Americans with Disabilities Act (ADA)<br>• Applies to other programs or activities available to the public that do NOT receive federal funds | |
| [Slide 1-33] Goals of Special Education<br>• Equality of opportunity<br>• Full participation<br>• Independent living<br>• Economic self-sufficiency<br>Measured by:<br>• High school completion rates<br>• Postschool employment rates<br>• Overall satisfaction with life | |

| | |
|---|---|
| [Slide 1-34] Looking to Thomas's Future<br>• The outlook for Thomas's future is bright, as seen in his parents' positive views of who he is and what he can accomplish.<br>• Thomas needs to be able to better access computers to aid in his life and learning.<br>• His parents envision Thomas continuing his education through college and finding a job that makes him happy.<br>• Their main goal for Thomas is that he reach his full potential | |

## Activities: Applying Your Learning

Just as the textbook described Universal Design for Learning as the way for you to teach children, the principles work well for adult learners too. Rather than just taking notes, taking quizzes, and writing essays, the following activities will help you to learn the material on a deeper level and remember it better.

1. Six principles of IDEA. Draw the six principles of IDEA. Though your drawings do not need to be artistic, make your drawings specific so you can recall each principle just from looking at the picture! Write down why each picture reminds you of the six principles.

| 1 | 2 | 3 |
|---|---|---|
| 4 | 5 | 6 |

2. Disability Laws. Fill in the two Venn diagrams below. Briefly write down the characteristics of each law in the corresponding circle. Where do the laws overlap? The overlapping parts should be written where the circles overlap.

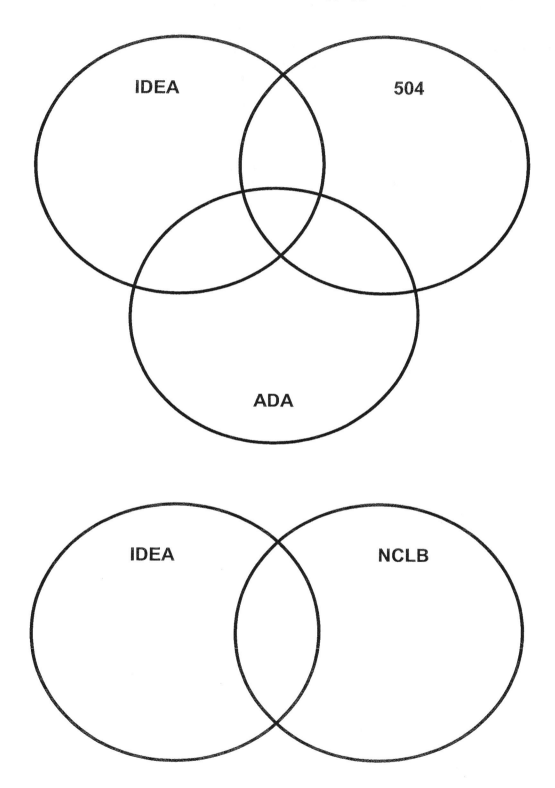

3. Other interactive activities are available at the Companion Website found at http://www.prenhall.com/turnbull. At the Companion Website you can see which famous people have disabilities and take a quiz to see if you can determine myths about individuals with disabilities. There are also video clips that illustrate an IEP mediation and how people with disabilities can be successful in the workplace. The best interactive experience is the STAR Legacy module on perceptions of disabilities.

4. Do not forget the DVD case studies packaged with your textbook. There you can see video clips of the individuals discussed in the book. While looking at the case studies in the *Real Lives & Exceptionalities* DVD, consider if IDEA's goals are reached by each individual featured in the segments in "Beyond School."

A good place to start is with Heather and Star Morgan. Their cases are discussed in Chapter 2. They are sisters in an incredible family. Barbara Morgan, their mother, has adopted several children with special needs into her family and has provided a warm and loving home for this diverse group of children.

*The questions that correspond to the DVD case studies are on the DVD but are also found in the back of this Student Study Guide. This will allow you to see the questions ahead of time. You are also welcome to write notes or answer the questions before typing them on the DVD.*

## Practice Quiz: Assessing Your Knowledge

Below are some questions to help you review the content in the chapter. Answers to the questions are provided for you at the end of the study guide. Circle the correct answer for each question.

1. One reason why more boys than girls receive special education services is:  PRAXIS 3     CEC 2
   A. Because there are more female teachers referring children for special education
   B. Because there has been an increase in single-mother families
   C. Because poverty has a greater influence on boys than girls
   D. Because fewer boys attend pre-school and pre-kindergarten programs

2. What is the current name for the 1975 law once known as PL 94:142?     PRAXIS 2     CEC 1
   A. Section 504
   B. The Americans with Disabilities Act
   C. No Child Left Behind Act
   D. The Individuals with Disabilities Education Act

3. Danny, who speaks Farsi, is given a psychological test in English. This violates which of the IDEA principles?
   PRAXIS 2              CEC 1
   A. Zero reject
   B. Nondiscriminatory evaluation
   C. Least restrictive environment
   D. Procedural due process

4. What is the largest category of students with disabilities? PRAXIS 1     CEC 1
   A. Speech and language impairments
   B. Learning disabilities
   C. Mental retardation
   D. Emotional disturbance

5. Instead of using labels such as "learning disabilities" or "mental retardation" to describe a child, what do the authors of our text suggest?     PRAXIS 3              CEC 1
   A. Use the child's name, such as "Mark"
   B. Use the child's grade level, such as "third grader"
   C. Use a statement of common ownership, such as "our student"
   D. Use the child's chronological age, such as "9-year-old"

6. An IFSP must be reviewed with family members:  PRAXIS 3              CEC 1
   A. Every 3 months
   B. Every 6 months
   C. Every 18 months
   D. Every 9 months

7. Which principle of IDEA requires that schools provide an individually tailored plan for every child with a disability? PRAXIS 2              CEC 1
   A. Zero reject
   B. Appropriate education
   C. Least restrictive environment
   D. Procedural due process

8. Which principle of IDEA requires that all children with disabilities be educated with students without disabilities to the maximum level appropriate for that child? PRAXIS 2              CEC 1
   A. Zero reject
   B. Appropriate education
   C. Least restrictive environment
   D. Procedural due process

9. Which of the following sequences of the 4-step process of nondiscriminatory evaluation is correct?
   PRAXIS 2           CEC 1
   A. Screening, referral, pre-referral, evaluation
   B. Pre-referral, referral, screening, evaluation
   C. Pre-referral, referral, evaluation, screening
   D. Screening, pre-referral, referral, evaluation

10. What is the purpose of a nondiscriminatory evaluation?    PRAXIS 2           CEC 1
    A. To ensure that students from all racial and ethnic groups can benefit from special education
    B. To determine if the child has a disability and the types of services he or she needs
    C. To ensure that diversity is practiced in all schools receiving federal special education funds
    D. To ensure that the child will be educated in the least restrictive environment

11. What span of ages is covered in Part B of IDEA?           PRAXIS 2           CEC 1
    A. Birth to age 2
    B. Ages 3 to 5
    C. Ages 3 to 21
    D. Ages 5 to 21

12. What does IDEA provide when a parent or state or local education agency disagree? PRAXIS 2     CEC 1
    A. An opportunity to engage in mediation
    B. Conflict resolution workshops at no charge
    C. A court appointed lawyer at no charge
    D. A choice of a different special education placement for the child

13. IFSP is an acronym for?          PRAXIS 2           CEC 1
    A. Individual Family Service Plan
    B. Infant Family Service Program
    C. Individual For Service Program
    D. Infant Family Service Plan

14. Which of the following describe the special education outcomes for students with disabilities?
    PRAXIS 3           CEC 2
    A. These students experience a high school graduation rate similar to those students without disabilities.
    B. These students experience employment rates similar to those students without disabilities.
    C. These students report overall life satisfaction at similar levels as compared to those without disabilities.
    D. None of the above

15. Which anti-discrimination law only applies to institutions that receive federal financial assistance?
    PRAXIS 2           CEC 1
    A. IDEA
    B. Section 504
    C. American with Disabilities Act
    D. No Child Left Behind

Now that you have completed your chapter study, go back to the chapter objectives and see if you have truly met them. You may want to write out your responses to the chapter objectives so that you can check your understanding against the chapter outline or the text.

# Chapter 2: Ensuring Progress in the General Curriculum Through Universal Design for Learning and Inclusion

## Objectives: Guiding Your Chapter Reading

The content in this chapter is presented to help you achieve the following objectives. Once you complete your study of the chapter, see if you can do what the objectives describe. If not, you may need to do some more reviewing of the chapter and your class notes.

- Describe how students with disabilities interact within systems of accountability
- Illustrate uses of universally designed learning
- Differentiate among various placement opportunities
- Recall key characteristics of inclusion
- Explain the importance of progressing through the general curriculum for students with disabilities

## Standards Matrices: Relating Content to Professional Standards

The matrices, or charts, below help you see how the professional standards from the Council for Exceptional Children (CEC) and PRAXIS™ apply to the content in this chapter. In addition, you can refer to the margin notes throughout the chapter and the activities at the end of each chapter to make sure you understand how these standards apply to the content in the field of special education. These standards are important for you to know, because they provide the basis for the professional teacher certification examinations and content covered in these exams.

| CEC Standards | Topic |
|---|---|
| 1 | • Standard-based reform<br>• Accountability issues<br>• Inclusion |
| 2 | • Case study<br>• Universal design for learning<br>• Restructuring teaching and learning |
| 3 | • Progressing in the general curriculum<br>• Inclusion<br>• Restructuring teaching and learning<br>• Assessment accommodations |
| 4 | • Progressing in the general curriculum<br>• Standard-based reform<br>• Universal design for learning |
| 5 | • Progressing in the general curriculum<br>• Accountability issues<br>• Universal design for learning |
| 6 | • Parent responses to inclusion |
| 7 | • Progressing in the general curriculum<br>• Universal design for learning<br>• Restructuring teaching and learning |
| 8 | • Progressing in the general curriculum<br>• Standard-based reform<br>• Accountability issues<br>• Universal design for learning |
| 9 | • Standard-based reform<br>• Accountability issues<br>• Inclusion<br>• Parent responses to inclusion |
| 10 | • Parent responses to inclusion |

| PRAXIS™ Standards | Topic |
|---|---|
| 1 | • Characteristics of inclusion<br>• Progressing in the general curriculum |
| 2 | • Standards-based reform<br>• Accountability issues |
| 3 | • Universal design for learning |

## Checking for Understanding: Key Terms

To check that you understand the basic terms and vocabulary in the chapter, use the space provided to write the definitions or descriptions in your own words. Then, check the chapter to see how accurate your definition is, making sure you understand the context, or situation, in which the word is used. Reviewing these terms will help you better understand the concepts that support the content in this chapter.

| Term | Definition/Description | (✓) |
|---|---|---|
| standards-based reform | | |
| academic content standards | | |
| student achievement standards | | |
| alternative achievement standards | | |
| general education curriculum | | |
| alternative assessment | | |
| supplementary aids and services | | |
| universal design for learning | | |
| specially designed instruction | | |

| Term | Definition/Description | (✓) |
|------|------------------------|-----|
| inclusion | | |
| mainstreaming | | |
| regular education initiative | | |
| continuum of placements | | |
| home-school placements | | |
| natural proportions | | |

## Chapter Outline: Taking Chapter Notes

The following outline is taken from the PowerPoint slides or overheads that your professor uses in class for this chapter. In the slides, there are several embedded links to more information for this chapter. Please go to the Companion Website at http://www.prenhall.com/turnbull to access them easily.

If you take your Student Study Guide to class, you can use this outline for taking notes on the chapter or for review. It will also allow you to listen to lectures and participate in class discussions without having to copy down all the PowerPoint information.

The notes below are set up for recording information from the chapter in a particular way—an adapted Cornell method of taking notes. In this adapted Cornell method, you underline, or highlight, information presented to you. In addition to highlighting, you can write information or explanations on the left-hand side of the table. Soon after the class presentation or reading the chapter, rewrite the notes from the left-hand side in your own words, using key terms and phrases. To study for quizzes or exams, you can cover up the left-hand side and use the right-hand side of the table to cue yourself about the information.

You also may just jot notes on the right-hand side to help you. Since this outline reduces the chapter for you, it will be a useful study aid. The summary at the end of the chapter is another useful resource to use for review.

| Chapter 2:<br>Ensuring Progress in the General Curriculum Through Universal Design for Learning and Inclusion | NOTES |
|---|---|
| [Slide 2-1] Chapter 2 Objectives: At the end of this chapter you should be able to:<br>• Describe how students with disabilities interact within systems of accountability<br>• Illustrate uses of universally designed learning<br>• Differentiate among various placement opportunities<br>• Recall key characteristics of inclusion<br>• Explain the importance of progressing through the general curriculum for students with disabilities | |
| [Slide 2-2] Who Are Heather and Star Morgan?<br>• Heather and Star are sisters; Heather is in the 3rd grade; Star is in the 1st grade.<br>• Both Heather and Star are adopted; both girls have mental retardation to differing degrees.<br>• Heather loves to read. In class, she reads in groups with her age-appropriate peers.<br>• Star is shy, yet shows a bright personality. She cannot speak verbally, but uses sign language, and the other first grade students can sign along.<br>• The school faculty is currently deciding if Heather will take the statewide assessment, and they will have to do this again when Star reaches third grade. | |
| [Slide 2-3] What Does Progressing In the General Curriculum Mean?<br>Assessing student progress:<br>• Toward specified outcomes based on standards in the general education curriculum | |
| [Slide 2-4] Standards-Based Reform<br>For many years:<br>• State and local education agencies did not have a clear curriculum for all students<br>• Teachers thought that students with disabilities should not participate nor be expected to master the general curriculum | |
| [Slide 2-5] Standards-Based Reform<br>• IDEA requires that students with disabilities participate AND show progress in the general curriculum<br>• The No Child Left behind Act (NCLB) overcomes low expectations by:<br>    ▪ Requiring states to establish content and performance standards for ALL students | |

| | |
|---|---|
| [Slide 2-6] Standards-Based Reform<br>• Academic Content Standards<br>    ▪ Define the knowledge, skills, and understanding that ALL students should attain in academic subjects<br>• Student Achievement Standards<br>    ▪ Define the level of achievement that students should meet in order to demonstrate proficiency in a subject<br>• States may establish alternative achievement standards<br>• For students with significant cognitive disabilities<br>• Must still align with academic content standards | |
| [Slide 2-7] Connecting the Curriculum to the Standards<br>• Establishes content and achievement standards<br>• Develops and implements a general curriculum based on content standards<br>• Assesses student progress in meeting the general curriculum's performance standards | |
| [Slide 2-8] Making Accommodations in Assessments<br>• IEP teams must consider any accommodations needed in the assessment process<br>• Accommodations that do not affect the content of the assessment include:<br>    ▪ Changes in presenting information<br>    ▪ Changes in responding<br>    ▪ Changes in timing<br>    ▪ Changes in setting | |
| [Slide 2-9] Making Accommodations in Assessments<br>• Alternative Assessments<br>    ▪ Determined by the IEP team<br>    ▪ For students who cannot perform on grade-level<br>    ▪ Aligned with the state subject area standards<br>    ▪ Serve the same purposes as the standard assessments:<br>        • Accountability<br>        • Decision-making | |
| [Slide 2-10] Making Accommodations in Assessments<br>• Students from diverse racial and ethnic backgrounds may be disadvantaged when it comes to assessments<br>• The research gives evidence that students from European or Asian backgrounds score higher than African American and Latino students | |

| | |
|---|---|
| [Slide 2-11] In Favor of Standards-Based Reform<br>• Comparable standards will result in higher expectations and higher levels of student achievement<br>• By being part of the standards process, students with disabilities will also be part of the education reform movement | |
| [Slide 2-12] Against Standards-Based Reform<br>• Holding students to the same standards can conflict with IEP goals<br>• Students will become frustrated, discouraged, and drop out of school | |
| [Slide 2-13] How Do Supplementary Aids and Services Support Progress?<br>• Aids, services, and other supports provided in general education classes or other education related settings to enable children with disabilities to be educated with non-disabled children to the maximum extent appropriate<br>• Considered non-instructional modifications and supports | |
| [Slide 2-14] Supplementary Aids and Services (See Figure 2–1) | |
| [Slide 2-15] What is Universal Design for Learning and How Does UDL Facilitate Progress?<br>• Universal design seeks to make learning accessible to all students<br>• Promotes flexibility in:<br>  • Representing content (curriculum materials)<br>  • Presenting content (instruction)<br>  • Demonstrating content mastery (evaluation)<br>• NIMAS standards<br>• Go to CAST for more information. | |
| [Slide 2-16] Placement Trends<br>(U.S. Department of Education Yearly Report)<br>• Increasing trend of including students with disabilities<br>• Students with milder disabilities are more likely to be included<br>• Elementary students are more likely to be included than high school students | |

| | |
|---|---|
| [Slide 2-17] Six Placement Categories (See Figure 2–4)<br>• Special education outside the regular classroom for less than 21% of the day<br>• Special education outside the regular classroom for more than 60% of the day<br>• Public separate facility<br>• Private separate facility<br>• Public residential facility<br>• Private residential facility | |
| [Slide 2-18] Special Education Environments: 2003–2004, Ages 6–21 (See Figure 2–5) | |
| [Slide 2-19] What Issues Are Related to Different Placements?<br>• Residential/home/hospital settings<br>• Special-school placements<br>• Specialized-settings placements within typical schools | |
| [Slide 2-20] Four Characteristics of Inclusion<br>• Home-school placement<br>• Principle of natural proportions<br>• Restructuring teaching and learning<br>• Age- and grade-appropriate placements<br>  Which includes:<br>      ▪ Eliminating the continuum of placements<br>      ▪ Increasing the amount of time students spend in general education classrooms | |
| [Slide 2-21] Research on Perspectives Toward Inclusion (See Figure 2–7)<br>• Educators' Perspectives<br>• Parents' Perspectives<br>• Students' Perspectives | |
| [Slide 2-22] Student Outcomes<br>• Positive outcomes<br>• Concerns<br>• Issues with research | |
| [Slide 2-23] How Does Inclusion Facilitate Progress?<br>• The general education classroom is where the general curriculum is most likely to be taught<br>• Students can receive individualized education in the general education classroom when UDL and the four characteristics of inclusion are met<br>• IDEA and NCLB have changed the focus on access to the general curriculum from "Where" to:<br>      • "What," a focus on what the student is taught (curriculum mastery)<br>            AND<br>      • "How," a focus on methods and pedagogy | |

| | |
|---|---|
| [Slide 2-24] Individualized Education Program<br>• Assure individualization<br>• The student's right to participate<br>• The student's right to make progress in the general curriculum<br>• The student's unique learning needs | |
| [Slide 2-25] Four "Must-Have" Components for IEPs<br>• Supplementary aids and services<br>• Special education services and specially designed services<br>• Other educational needs that must be met in order to make progress in the general education classroom<br>• Related services | |
| [Slide 2-26] IEP Decision Making Progress (See Figure 2–8) | |
| [Slide 2-27] What Should Educators Do to Support Progress?<br>• Create learning communities<br>• Design units and lessons<br>• Cognitive taxonomies<br>• Implement school-wide instructional strategies | |
| [Slide 2-28] Looking to Star's and Heather's Future<br>• Heather can live on her own as an adult and be economically self-sufficient.<br>• She will have friends, the same opportunities as those friends to participate in community life, and have equal opportunities.<br>• Star will also live and work in the community, but with more supports.<br>• She may live in a group home with other adults.<br>• She will also have friends in the community.<br>• Continued access to the general curriculum will allow them to live out these goals. | |

## Activities: Applying Your Learning

Just as the textbook described Universal Design for Learning as the way for you to teach children, the principles work well for adult learners too. Rather than just taking notes, taking quizzes, and writing essays, the following activities will help you to learn the material on a deeper level and remember it better.

1. Universal Design for Learning. There are many ways to present and many ways to respond that improve learning. Let's see how creative you are! How many ways can you present material to your students (there is always lecture, but material could be taught through interpretive dance)? How many ways could your students respond (besides tests or papers they could create a song or a draw the story board to a commercial)? Let's compete with your peers; using another piece of paper, who can write the longest list?

2. Write a personal IEP for yourself. Even though you do not necessarily have identified special needs, we all have learning preferences and styles in how we like to learn. Use your own learning preferences to plan your individualized instructional plan for learning in this class on the prepared sheet on the next page.. (Note: This is not really like a full IEP. You are missing many parts of it, including goals and objectives. See Figure 1–7 for all of the required contents. But this will give you the main idea.)

**Individualized Education Plan for: Name_____**

- *Identify the supplementary aids and services you need*:
(Do you need notebook supplies? Writing instruments? Books? Study buddy? Instructor phone number, email and/or office hours? Make a list of all of the supplies you need to be successful)

- *Identify the special education services or specially designed instruction you need.*
(Do you prefer lecture? Hands-on assignments? Reading? Computer activities? The textbook provides many multimedia options for learning the material. Which methods work best for you?)

- *Identify your other educational needs.*
(Do you have other concerns that need addressing to be successful in this class? Though not addressed in the curriculum of this course, have you already figured out transportation, parking, computer access, time management, or other non academic considerations?)

- *Identify the related services you need to be educated in this class.*

3. Other interactive activities are available at the Companion Website found at http://www.prenhall.com/turnbull. On the Companion Website, there are some informative STAR Legacy Modules to explain the impact of high-stakes testing and special education students. There is also an interesting activity from CAST to demonstrate Universal Design for Learning principles.

4. Do not forget the DVD Cases that come with your textbook. There you can see video clips of the individuals discussed in the book.

Have you looked at the clips involving Heather and Star Morgan? Their cases are discussed in Chapter 2. They are sisters in an incredible family. Barbara Morgan, their mother, has adopted several children with special needs and has provided a warm and loving home for this diverse group of children.

After viewing the cases on Star and Heather on the *Real Lives & Exceptionalities* DVD, answer the following:

How are Star and Heather's needs the same?

How are Star and Heather's needs different?

After viewing Clip 9 (MeMe) under "Beyond School" on the *Real Lives & Exceptionalities* DVD, what examples do you see of Universal Design and assistive technologies?

*The questions that correspond to the DVD case studies are on the DVD but are also found in the back of this Student Study Guide. This will allow you to see the questions ahead of time. You are also welcomd to write notes or answer the questions before typing them on the DVD.*

## Practice Quiz: Assessing Your Knowledge

Below are some questions to help you review the content in the chapter. Answers to the questions are provided for you at the end of the study guide. Circle the correct answer for each question.

1. The field of architecture inspired which of the following educational designs?     PRAXIS 3     CEC 3
   - A. Direct Instruction
   - B. Indirect Instruction
   - C. Universal Design
   - D. None of the above

2. What is the fundamental contribution of universal design?     PRAXIS 3     CEC 3
   - A. To tailor teaching, learning, and assessment to the needs of the students
   - B. To determine if the child has a disability and, if so, to determine the least restrictive environment for that child
   - C. To help teachers collaborate on behalf of all students in the general education environment
   - D. To maintain the same academic expectations for all students, regardless of their learning ability

3. What is the name of the law Congress enacted in 2001 that applies to all students in all schools?
   PRAXIS 2          CEC 1
   - A. IDEA
   - B. No Child Left Behind
   - C. ADA
   - D. Section 504

4. Which term below defines the knowledge, skills, and understandings that students should attain in core subjects?     PRAXIS 3          CEC 3
   - A. Academic performance standards
   - B. Academic content standards
   - C. Instructional design standards
   - D. Universal design for learning

5. Which of the following is NOT and example of inclusion practice?     PRAXIS 3          CEC 3
   - A. Ms. Bosey allows a student to use a calculator to complete a math activity.
   - B. Mr. Jaso provides a student with a book at a lower reading level that covers the same material.
   - C. Mrs. Myra assigns a middle school student to the neighboring elementary school to receive math instruction on his grade level.
   - D. Mr. James allows a student to make an illustration (rather than a book report) to show that she comprehends a book chapter.

6. What is one disadvantage of the standards-based reform movement for students with disabilities?
   PRAXIS 3          CEC 8
   - A. These students will no longer be placed in the least restrictive environment.
   - B. These students' IEPs will need to be rewritten with higher expectations.
   - C. These students will be frustrated, discouraged, and drop out.
   - D. These students will no longer generate funds for special education.

7. Which of the following is NOT a testing accommodation?     PRAXIS 3          CEC 8
   - A. Making a change in the test setting
   - B. Making a change in the test response mode
   - C. Making a change in the test content
   - D. Making a change in the test presentation

8. Which phase of inclusion attempted to unite general and special education into one system?
   PRAXIS 3                     CEC 7
   A. Mainstreaming
   B. Regular education initiative
   C. Inclusion through accommodations
   D. Inclusion through restructuring

9. When discussing the principle of natural proportions, what is the maximum percentage of students with disabilities that should be enrolled in a general education classroom, as suggested by Walther-Thomas and her colleagues? PRAXIS 3            CEC 1
   A. 9%
   B. 10%
   C. 20%
   D. 30%

10. What positive benefit did students with disabilities mention about special education, according to the research cited in this chapter? PRAXIS 3            CEC 5
    A. Special education allowed for more opportunities for making friends
    B. Special education had more enjoyable activities
    C. Special education helped them meet their identified IEP needs
    D. Special education helped them pass required state and local exams

11. Which group tends to be the most positive about inclusion?          PRAXIS 3            CEC 10
    A. Students with disabilities
    B. Parents of students with disabilities
    C. General educators
    D. The general public

12. Which students are given alternative testing on high-stakes standardized tests?      PRAXIS 3     CEC 3
    A. Students who do not take tests well due to test anxiety but read on grade level
    B. Students who have mild learning disabilities but are unable to take tests due to their disability
    C. General education classroom students who have previously scored low and need alternative testing procedures
    D. Students who are not able to complete work on the least complex entry point

13. Which two issues tend to be the most controversial regarding inclusion?     PRAXIS 3         CEC 3
    A. Eliminating the continuum of placements and increasing the amount of time students spend in general education
    B. Eliminating the need for IEPs and eliminating the continuum of placements
    C. Requiring all students to take state tests and requiring all students to have greater access to the general education curriculum
    D. Requiring all students to take state tests and eliminating the need for IEPs

14. With support and services coming to the student in the classroom, the student is more likely to:
    PRAXIS 3                     CEC 5
    A. Feel embarrassed to have others come to her
    B. Feel singled out and overwhelmed
    C. Feel empowered that others are coming to her
    D. Improve her social interaction skills

15. Placement of students with disabilities in inclusive settings compromised the performance of which group of students? PRAXIS 3            CEC 5
    A. Students without disabilities
    B. Students with IQs between 75 and 90
    C. Students with social skills problems
    D. None of the above

Now that you have completed your chapter study, go back to the chapter objectives and see if you have truly met them. You may want to write out your responses to the chapter objectives so that you can check your understanding against the chapter outline or the text.

# Chapter 3: Today's Multicultural, Bilingual, and Diverse Schools

## Objectives: Guiding Your Chapter Reading

The content in this chapter is presented to help you achieve the following objectives. Once you complete your study of the chapter, see if you can do what the objectives describe. If not, you may need to do some more reviewing of the chapter and your class notes.

- Describe the social impact of culture on special education
- Articulate issues impacting students from diverse backgrounds
- Critique evaluation processes for students from diverse backgrounds
- Describe practices used to include students from diverse backgrounds into the general curriculum

## Standards Matrices: Relating Content to Professional Standards

The matrices, or charts, below help you see how the professional standards from the Council for Exceptional Children (CEC) and PRAXIS™ apply to the content in this chapter. In addition, you can refer to the margin notes throughout the chapter and the activities at the end of each chapter to make sure you understand how these standards apply to the content in the field of special education. These standards are important for you to know, because they provide the basis for the professional teacher certification examinations and content covered in these exams.

| CEC Standards | Topic |
|---|---|
| 1 | <ul><li>Definition of culture</li><li>Social context of special education</li><li>History of special education</li><li>Cultural differences theories</li><li>Judicial cases</li><li>Disproportionate representation</li><li>Current trends and issues</li></ul> |
| 2 | <ul><li>Case study</li></ul> |
| 3 | <ul><li>Culturally responsive practices</li></ul> |
| 4 | <ul><li>Current trends and issues</li></ul> |
| 5 | <ul><li>Technical dimension of culturally responsive practice</li></ul> |
| 6 | |
| 7 | <ul><li>Technical dimension of culturally responsive practice</li></ul> |
| 8 | <ul><li>Evaluation and assessment</li><li>Ongoing monitoring</li></ul> |
| 9 | <ul><li>Culturally responsive professional</li></ul> |
| 10 | <ul><li>Partnership in the schools</li></ul> |

| PRAXIS™ Standards | Topic |
|---|---|
| 1 | <ul><li>Case study</li></ul> |
| 2 | <ul><li>Definition of culture</li><li>Social context of special education</li><li>History of special education</li><li>Cultural differences theories</li><li>Judicial cases</li><li>Disproportionate representation</li><li>Current trends and issues</li></ul> |
| 3 | <ul><li>Current trends and issues</li><li>Culturally responsive practices</li><li>Technical dimension of culturally responsive practice</li><li>Partnership in the schools</li></ul> |

## Checking for Understanding: Key Terms

To check that you understand the basic terms and vocabulary in the chapter, use the space provided to write the definitions or descriptions in your own words. Then, check the chapter to see how accurate your definition is, making sure you understand the context, or situation, in which the word is used. Reviewing these terms will help you better understand the concepts that support the content in this chapter.

| Term | Definition/Description | (✓) |
|---|---|---|
| genetic deficit theories | | |
| cultural deficit theory | | |
| cultural difference theory | | |
| **Additional Terms** | | |
| multicultural education | | |
| cultural diversity | | |
| disproportionate overrepresentation | | |
| culturally responsive practice | | |
| bilingual education | | |
| transitional bilingual education | | |
| maintenance bilingual education | | |
| English as a second language | | |
| immersion | | |

| Term | Definition/Description | (✓) |
|---|---|---|
| | | |
| sheltered English | | |
| submersion | | |
| **Court Cases** | | |
| *Brown v. Board of Education* (1954) | | |
| *Diana v. Board of Education* (1973) | | |
| *Larry P. v. Riles* (1972) | | |
| *PASE v. Hannon* (1980) | | |

## Chapter Outline: Taking Chapter Notes

The following outline is taken from the PowerPoint slides or overheads that your professor uses in class for this chapter. In the slides, there are several embedded links to more information for this chapter. Please go to the Companion Website at: http://www.prenhall.com/turnbull to access them easily.

If you take your Student Study Guide to class, you can use this outline for taking notes on the chapter or for review. It will also allow you to listen to lectures and participate in class discussions without having to copy down all the PowerPoint information.

The notes below are set up for recording information from the chapter in a particular way—an adapted Cornell method of taking notes. In this adapted Cornell method, you underline, or highlight, information presented to you. In addition to highlighting, you can write information or explanations on the left-hand side of the table. Soon after the class presentation or reading the chapter, rewrite the notes from the left-hand side in your own words, using key terms and phrases. To study for quizzes or exams, you can cover up the left-hand side and use the right-hand side of the table to cue yourself about the information.

You also may just jot notes on the right-hand side to help you. Since this outline reduces the chapter for you, it will be a useful study aid. The summary at the end of the chapter is another useful resource to use for review.

| Chapter 3<br>Today's Multicultural, Bilingual, and Diverse Schools | NOTES |
|---|---|
| [Slide 3-1] Chapter 3 Objectives: At the end of this chapter you should be able to:<br>• Describe the social impact of culture on special education<br>• Articulate issues impacting students from diverse backgrounds<br>• Critique evaluation processes for students from diverse backgrounds<br>• Describe practices used to include students from diverse backgrounds into the general curriculum | |
| [Slide 3-2] Who is Joesian Cortes?<br>• A 17-year-old 11th grade student in Brooklyn<br>• Parents from Puerto Rico; mother speaks only Spanish; both Joesian and father speak Spanish and English<br>• Joesian describes himself as a "non-reader"<br>• His mother says that teachers knew he couldn't read, yet overlooked it, and promoted him<br>• His family wonders if he was the victim of cultural discrimination<br>• They work with advocates at United We Stand of New York, a community-based resource center for traditionally underserved/unserved families and students<br>• Joesian has many positive attributes: he switches easily from one language to another; is an eager, sincere, and kind student; defers to his elders and teachers; is not a troublemaker; and is not likely to draw attention to himself | |
| [Slide 3-3] Culture and the Schools<br>• Culture is the customary beliefs, social norms, and material traits of a racial, religious, or social group; a shared way of life<br>    ■ four key points:<br>        – Embodies a historical component<br>        – Is a resource for daily life<br>        – Is associated with, but not limited to, particular locations in which people interact over time<br>        – Exists in everyday context | |
| [Slide 3-4] Four Aspects of Culture<br>1. The practices of the cultural group to which the student belongs<br>2. The group's history<br>3. The particular child's history<br>4. The culturally expected roles, goals, resources, constraints, tensions, beliefs, and biases of the individuals who have shaped and who now participate in the student's community, school, and classroom<br>    • Culture is a reciprocal phenomenon; educators transmit it to their students and the students respond in turn | |

| | |
|---|---|
| [Slide 3-5] The Social Context of Special Education<br>• History before IDEA:<br>    • Theories about genetic and cultural deficits<br>    • Re-emerged in the 1990s with *The Bell Curve*<br>    • Theories about cultural differences<br>• Different theories resulted in different responses by schools and school systems | |
| [Slide 3-6] School System Responses<br>• The common school<br>• Treatment of second- and third-generation European Americans, immigrant students, and African Americans<br>• Tracking practices<br>• School segregation<br>• Civil rights movement<br>• Desegregation resulted in high numbers of students from culturally and linguistically diverse backgrounds being increasingly tracked into programs for students with mental retardation | |
| [Slide 3-7] Enactment and Implementation of IDEA<br>• Did IDEA dismantle discrimination against students from diverse backgrounds?<br>    ▪ *Larry P. v. Riles* (1972, 1974)<br>    ▪ *PASE v. Hannon* (1980) | |
| [Slide 3-8] Overrepresentation<br>• In 1997, Congress amended IDEA to require state agencies to:<br>    ▪ Assess the efficacy of educational and transitional services for students with disabilities from diverse backgrounds<br>    ▪ Provide annual data about students from diverse backgrounds<br>    ▪ Intervene in school districts with significant overrepresentation | |
| [Slide 3-9] The Children's Defense Fund (2004)<br>• Classes in high poverty schools are 77% more likely to be assigned to an out-of-field teacher than are classes in low-poverty schools<br>• White schools are 60 percent less likely to be assigned out-of-field teachers than majority non-white schools<br>• Teachers with master's degrees are less likely to teach in high-minority, low-income schools than they are to teach in high-income, low-minority schools | |
| [Slide 3-10] Evaluating Students from Culturally and Linguistically Diverse Backgrounds<br>• First step is prereferral, where educators should ask:<br>    ▪ What do we think about our student(s) and their home and community environments?<br>    ▪ On what do we base these beliefs?<br>    ▪ Might our beliefs be based on stereotypes?<br>    ▪ How will these stereotypes affect our interactions with these students?<br>• IDEA requires non-discriminatory evaluation | |

| | |
|---|---|
| [Slide 3-11] Using Effective Instructional Strategies<br>• Culturally responsive teaching practices<br>  http://www.schoolredesign.net/srn/server.php?idx=886racti<br>  ces<br>• Includes personal dimensions, technical dimensions, and<br>  institutional practices<br>• Personal dimension includes:<br>  ▪ The teacher's own biography<br>  ▪ The teacher's beliefs about culture, learning, and<br>    teaching<br>  ▪ The school and classroom contexts in which the<br>    teacher has learned and practices<br>  ▪ The teacher's professional development activities | |
| [Slide 3-12] Classroom Characteristics<br>• Nurturing and supportive social environment<br>• Community of learners<br>• Fluid and spontaneous social interactions<br>• Teacher's beliefs<br>• Other factors? | |
| [Slide 3-13] Responsive Pedagogy for Ethnically Diverse<br>Students<br>• Includes transformative teaching<br>• Characterized by a curriculum organized around:<br>  ▪ Powerful ideas<br>  ▪ Highly interactive teaching strategies<br>  ▪ Active student involvement<br>  ▪ Personal, social and civic activities | |
| [Slide 3-14] Who Are Linguistically Diverse Students?<br>• Substantial exposure to a social environment in which<br>  English is not the primary language<br>• Have acquired the communicative abilities of that social<br>  environment<br>• Are first exposed to a predominantly English-speaking<br>  environment when they begin their formal educational<br>  careers<br>• Heterogeneous group with over 100 languages in American<br>  public school systems (largest group: Latino ancestry)<br>• Are learning difficulties due to limited-English proficiency<br>  or a disability?<br>• This results in both overreferrals and underreferrals | |
| [Slide 3-15] Bilingual Special Education<br>• Designed to help each student maximize learning potential<br>• Programs include:<br>  ▪ Transitional bilingual education (widely used)<br>  ▪ Maintenance bilingual education (widely used)<br>  ▪ English as a second language<br>  ▪ Immersion<br>  ▪ Sheltered English<br>  ▪ Submersion | |

| | |
|---|---|
| [Slide 3-16] Institutional Dimension of Culturally Responsive Pedagogy (See Figure 3–7)<br>• Collective Responsibility<br>• Social Justice<br>• Theories about competence and difference<br>• Communities of Practice<br>• Maximize Teacher Learning<br>• Professional Development | |
| [Slide 3-17] Including Students from Culturally and Linguistically Diverse Backgrounds (See Partnership Tips, p. 74)<br>• Partnerships in schools<br>• Four questions to ask in developing a sound partnership<br>    ▪ Who?<br>    ▪ Why?<br>    ▪ How?<br>    ▪ Where? | |
| [Slide 3-18] Assessing Students in a Culturally Responsive Manner<br>• The Cultural Inquiry Process<br>• Use various assessments, not just standardized assessments<br>• Analyze assessments in a culturally responsive manner | |
| [Slide 3-19] Looking to Joesian's Future<br>• Joesian's allies will contribute to a successful future<br>• He wants to enter his uncle's trade, although, if possible, he'd like even more to become a firefighter<br>• To enter the trade, he must be able to pass a license examination in English<br>• In this way, it is clear that culture will continue to play a role in Joesian's future outside school | |

## Activities: Applying Your Learning

Just as the textbook described Universal Design for Learning as the way for you to teach children, the principles work well for adult learners too. Rather than just taking notes, taking quizzes, and writing essays, the following activities will help you to learn the material on a deeper level and remember it better.

1. Cultural Inquiry. Check your cultural assumptions! Jot your answers in the space below. Then pick out a partner to discuss either item a, b, or c.

| a) Do you expect students to make eye contact with you? How about if you are upset with them? Do you make eye contact with a person who is upset with you? How will you handle a student who reacts differently than you? | b) Do you expect students to work competitively or cooperatively? How do you prefer to work? How will you handle a student who learns differently than you? | c) Do you expect your students to confide in you? What if it is about another student? Do you confide in your instructors? How will you handle a student who is different than you? |
| --- | --- | --- |
|  |  |  |

After discussing the issue with your partner, think about this:
Did you both agree on how you would answer each question? What dangers are there of a teacher believing that his or her students are like he or she is?

2. Computer activity. (Links are available at the Companion Website at http://www.prehall.com/turnbull) On another piece of paper or on a word processing program, write a letter to the parent of a student who speaks another language. Describe to the parents their rights under IDEA.
Please include information from Chapter 1. Additional information can be found at: *Rights and Responsibilities of Parents of Children with Disabilities: Update 1999* http://ericec.org/digests/e575.html.

Type your letter (or copy and paste it) at Babel Fish Translation at http://babelfish.altavista.com/ to translate it to the language of the student's parents. Would this be a useful tool for communication?

3. Other interactive activities are available at the Companion Website found at http://www.prenhall.com/turnbull. An excellent STAR Legacy Module called "Teachers at the Loom" will give you a fresh experience in understanding different cultures and their impact on education.

4. Do not forget the DVD cases packaged with your textbook. There you can see video clips of the individuals discussed in the book.

To meet a bilingual teaching assistant who also has an exceptionality, visit Jael (Clip 1) under "Beyond School" on the *Real Lives & Exceptionalities* DVD.

After viewing the clip, think about how Jael's bilingualism has been an asset to her in her life as well in her ability to assist children. Write down some of your ideas.

*The questions that correspond to the DVD case studies are on the DVD but are also found in the back of this Student Study Guide. This will allow you to see the questions ahead of time. You are also welcome to write notes or answer the questions before typing them on the DVD.*

## Practice Quiz: Assessing Your Knowledge

Below are some questions to help you review the content in the chapter. Answers to the questions are provided for you at the end of the study guide. Circle the correct answer for each question.

1. What three factors influence culture?　　PRAXIS 3　　　　CEC 3
   - A. History, location, education
   - B. History, resource, location
   - C. History, resource, education
   - D. Resource, location, education

2. When making pre-referral decisions for students from diverse backgrounds, the team should use which of the following?　　PRAXIS 3　　　　CEC 8
   - A. Cultural Inquiry Process
   - B. Cultural Instructional Process
   - C. Cultural Process
   - D. Cultural Tests

3. Classes that have a disproportionate representation of students from culturally and linguistically diverse backgrounds are:　　PRAXIS 3　　　　CEC 3
   - A. Classes for students with mild mental retardation
   - B. Classes for students with moderate mental retardation
   - C. Classes for students with hearing impairments
   - D. None of the above

4. One court case that was instrumental in systemically addressing problems related to nondiscriminatory assessment was:　　PRAXIS 2　　　　CEC 1
   - A. *Diana v. Board of Education*
   - B. *Roe v. Wade*
   - C. *Timothy R. v Rochester*
   - D. *Tech Act*

5. Educators need constantly to consider their personal and collective histories because which of the following might happen if not addressed?　　PRAXIS 3　　　　CEC 1
   - A. A student's right to due process might be at risk
   - B. A student's right to individualized education planning participation might be at risk
   - C. A student's right to private education might be at risk
   - D. A student's right to a free appropriate public education might be at risk

6. What happens to students from diverse backgrounds when a teacher uses the lecture method?　　PRAXIS 3　　　　CEC 5
   - A. The students become engaged in the learning process
   - B. The students become cooperative learners
   - C. The students tend to drop out
   - D. The students have a low rate of academic engagement

7. When teachers are intent on building a community of learners and stimulating collaboration and self-regulation in their students, they develop what type of classroom?　　PRAXIS 3　　　　CEC 9
   - A. Ethnic
   - B. Culturally responsive
   - C. Culturally biased
   - D. None of the above

8. The primary purpose of bilingual special education is to help each individual student:  PRAXIS 3     CEC 3
    A. Learn English
    B. Overcome his or her disability
    C. To learn about his or her culture
    D. Achieve a maximum potential for learning

9. Which of the following is not an appropriate program for students who are learning English?
    PRAXIS 3              CEC 4
    A. Transitional bilingual education
    B. Maintenance bilingual education
    C. English as a second language
    D. Special education

10. Which group of students is overrepresented in the gifted program?          PRAXIS 1          CEC 2
    A. Hispanics
    B. Pacific Islanders
    C. Native Americans
    D. African Americans

11. The Children's Defense Fund (2004) reported the number of children who live in poverty at:
    PRAXIS 1                CEC 2
    A. 1 in 6
    B. 2 in 8
    C. Less than 50%
    D. There is no exact number

12. Which of the following statements is true?        PRAXIS 3             CEC 1
    A. Teachers with masters degrees are more likely to teach in high-minority, low-income schools
    B. Teachers with masters degrees are less likely to teach in high-minority, low-income schools
    C. Teachers with masters degrees teach only in high-income, low-minority schools
    D. Teachers with masters degrees are more likely to teach in private schools

13. A failure of the school system is which of the following?  PRAXIS 3             CEC 3
    A. Failure to meet the needs of students from diverse backgrounds
    B. Failure to meet the needs of students in the gifted program
    C. Failure to meet the needs of students in special education
    D. Failure to meet the needs of all children

14. Teachers should take into account which of the following:        PRAXIS 2          CEC 3
    A. Students come from all types of backgrounds
    B. Their own biases
    C. A and B
    D. None of the above

15. Parent participation is a principle of:     PRAXIS 2          CEC 1
    A. NCLB
    B. IDEA
    C. Nondiscriminatory evaluation
    D. Tech Act

Now that you have completed your chapter study, go back to the chapter objectives and see if you have truly met them. You may want to write out your responses to the chapter objectives so that you can check your understanding against the chapter outline or the text.

# Chapter 4: Today's Families and Their Partnerships with Professionals

## Objectives: Guiding Your Chapter Reading

The content in this chapter is presented to help you achieve the following objectives. Once you complete your study of the chapter, see if you can do what the objectives describe. If not, you may need to do some more reviewing of the chapter and your class notes.

- Describe the characteristics of today's families
- Articulate the importance of partnerships
- Identify the five components of families' quality of life and the role of the educator
- Illustrate the seven principles of creating successful partnerships

## Standards Matrices: Relating Content to Professional Standards

The matrices, or charts, below help you see how the professional standards from the Council for Exceptional Children (CEC) and PRAXIS™ apply to the content in this chapter. In addition, you can refer to the margin notes throughout the chapter and the activities at the end of each chapter to make sure you understand how these standards apply to the content in the field of special education. These standards are important for you to know because they provide the basis for the professional teacher certification examinations and content covered in these exams.

| CEC Standards | Topic |
|---|---|
| 1 | • Role of special educator |
| 2 | • Characteristics of families and partnerships<br>• Quality of life as it relates to families and their children with exceptionalities<br>• Sibling relationships |
| 3 | |
| 4 | |
| 5 | |
| 6 | |
| 7 | |
| 8 | |
| 9 | • Role of special educator |
| 10 | • Case study<br>• Collaboration<br>• Forming relationships with families<br>• Removal of barriers for partnership<br>• Communication |

| PRAXIS™ Standards | Topic |
|---|---|
| 1 | • Case study<br>• Characteristics of families and partnerships<br>• Quality of life as it relates to families and their children with exceptionalities<br>• Sibling relationships |
| 2 | • Role of special educator |
| 3 | • Role of special educator<br>• Collaboration<br>• Forming relationships with families<br>• Removal of barriers for partnership<br>• Communication |

## Checking for Understanding: Key Terms

To check that you understand the basic terms and vocabulary in the chapter, use the space provided to write the definitions or descriptions in your own words. Then, check the chapter to see how accurate your definition is, making sure you understand the context, or situation, in which the word is used. Reviewing these terms will help you better understand the concepts that support the content in this chapter.

| Term | Definition/Description | (✓) |
|---|---|---|
| family | | |
| kinship care | | |
| family-professional partnership | | |
| domains of family life | | |
| family quality of life | | |
| Circle of Friends | | |
| self-determination | | |
| advocacy | | |
| skilled dialogue | | |
| anchored understanding | | |
| third space | | |
| **Court Cases** | | |

| Term | Definition/Description | (✓) |
|---|---|---|
| *Mills v. DC Board of Education* (1972) | | |
| *PARC v. Commonwealth* (1991, 1992) | | |
| *Irving Independent School District v. Tatro* (1984) | | |
| *Cedar Rapids v. Garrott F.* (1999) | | |
| *Board of Education v. Rowley* (1982) | | |

## Chapter Outline: Taking Chapter Notes

The following outline is taken from the PowerPoint slides or overheads that your professor uses in class for this chapter. In the slides, there are several embedded links to more information for this chapter. Please go to the Companion Website at http://www.prenhall.com/turnbull to access them easily.

If you take your Student Study Guide to class, you can use this outline for taking notes on the chapter or for review. It will also allow you to listen to lectures and participate in class discussions without having to copy down all the PowerPoint information.

The notes below are set up for recording information from the chapter in a particular way—an adapted Cornell method of taking notes. In this adapted Cornell method, you underline, or highlight, information presented to you. In addition to highlighting, you can write information or explanations on the left-hand side of the table. Soon after the class presentation or reading the chapter, rewrite the notes from the left-hand side in your own words, using key terms and phrases. To study for quizzes or exams, you can cover up the left-hand side and use the right-hand side of the table to cue yourself about the information.

You also may just jot notes on the right-hand side to help you. Since this outline reduces the chapter for you, it will be a useful study aid. The summary at the end of the chapter is another useful resource to use for review.

| Chapter 4: Today's Families and Their Partnerships with Professionals | NOTES |
|---|---|
| [Slide 4-1] Chapter 4 Objectives: At the end of this chapter you should be able to:<br>• Describe the characteristics of today's families<br>• Articulate the importance of partnerships<br>• Identify the five components of families' quality of life and the role of the educator<br>• Illustrate the seven principles of creating successful partnerships | |

| | |
|---|---|
| [Slide 4-2] Who Is the Holley Family?<br>• The Holleys are a military family<br>• Sean, 12 years old, has autism and epilepsy and JT, 14 years old, has learning disabilities and is also in gifted education<br>• Father Jamie's military job, with extra tours of duty without his family, has presented some parental difficulties<br>• He takes extra tours of duty in return for assurances from the Army that his family can stay in Kansas, where his sons receive an excellent education<br>• Sean's mom, Leia, and his teacher, Tierney, have good and bad times in their partnership<br>• Sean has now transitioned to middle school | |
| [Slide 4-3] Who Are Today's Families?<br>• Definitions of "family"<br>• U.S. Census Bureau: A group of two or more people related by birth, marriage, or adoption who reside together<br>• Authors: Two or more people who regard themselves to be a family and who carry out the functions that families typically perform | |
| [Slide 4-4] Who Are Today's Families?<br>• Similarities among families with and without disabilities<br>• Differences among families with and without disabilities<br>    ▪ Income<br>    ▪ Education level<br>    ▪ Household composition | |
| [Slide 4-5] What Are Partnerships and Why Are They Important?<br>• Family-professional partnerships—families and professional collaborate with each other, capitalizing on each other's judgment and expertise to the benefit of the student<br>• Partnerships are important because they:<br>    ▪ Foster trust<br>    ▪ Stimulate student achievement<br>    ▪ Enhance families' quality of life | |
| [Slide 4-6] How Do Children with Exceptionalities Affect Their Families' Quality of Life?<br>• Mothers' stress and depression when raising a child with a disability<br>• Findings are mixed<br>• Mothers who have children with certain types of disabilities (such as those with behavioral problems or intense caretaking needs) have greater stress | |

| | |
|---|---|
| **[Slide 4-7] Domains of Family Quality of Life**<br>• The authors have identified five domains of family quality of life:<br>  ▪ Emotional well-being<br>  ▪ Parenting<br>  ▪ Family interaction<br>  ▪ Physical/material well-being<br>  ▪ Disability-related support | |
| **[Slide 4-8] Emotional Well-Being**<br>• Families experience better emotional well-being when:<br>  ▪ Friends or others provide support<br>  ▪ They receive the support they need to relieve stress<br>  ▪ They have time to pursue their own interests<br>  ▪ Outside help is available to take care of the special needs of all family members | |
| **[Slide 4-9] Positive Approaches**<br>• Utilize Circle of Friends<br>• Encourage parents to be involved with other parents<br>• Be available to parents outside regular school hours | |
| **[Slide 4-10] Parenting**<br>• Parenting is strong when families can help their child:<br>  ▪ Learn to be independent<br>  ▪ With schoolwork and activities<br>  •Get along with others<br>  ▪ With individual needs | |
| **[Slide 4-11] Self-Determination**<br>• Self-determination—acting as the primary causal agent in one's life and making choices and decisions regarding one's quality of life free from undue external influence or interference<br>http://www.pacer.org/tatra/self.htm<br>• Characteristics of self-determination:<br>  ▪ The student acts autonomously<br>  ▪ The student's behavior is self-regulated<br>  ▪ The student acts in a psychologically empowered manner in initiating and responding to events<br>  ▪ The student acts in a self-realizing manner | |
| **[Slide 4-12] Family Interaction**<br>• Families who have high levels of family interaction:<br>  ▪ Enjoy spending time together<br>  ▪ Talk openly with each other<br>  ▪ Solve problems together<br>  ▪ Show they love and care for each other | |
| **[Slide 4-13] Physical/Material Well-Being**<br>• This can include the ability of families to:<br>  ▪ Access transportation<br>  ▪ Pay expenses<br>  ▪ Feel safe at home, work, school, and in the neighborhood<br>  ▪ Obtain medical and dental help when needed | |

| | |
|---|---|
| [Slide 4-14] Disability-Related Support<br>• Some aspects of disability-related support help the student to:<br>    ▪ Achieve goals at school or work<br>    ▪ Make progress at home<br>    ▪ Make friends<br>    ▪ Have a good relationship between family and service providers | |
| [Slide 4-15] How Can You Form Partnerships with Families?<br>• Partnerships build on the strengths, talents, resources, and expertise of educators, families, and others<br>• Seven principles of partnerships:<br>    ▪ Communication<br>    ▪ Professional Competence<br>    ▪ Respect<br>    ▪ Commitment<br>    ▪ Equality<br>    ▪ Advocacy<br>    ▪ Trust | |
| [Slide 4-16] Communication<br>    • Five practices for effective communication:<br>    ▪ Be friendly<br>    ▪ Listen<br>    ▪ Be clear<br>    ▪ Be honest<br>    ▪ Provide and coordinate information<br>    • Three major networks of parent programs:<br>    ▪ Parent Training and Information Centers<br>    ▪ Community Parent Resource Centers<br>    ▪ Parent to Parent Programs | |
| [Slide 4-17] Professional Competence<br>• Three practices associated with professional competence:<br>    ▪ Provide a quality education<br>    ▪ Continue to learn<br>    ▪ Set high expectations | |
| [Slide 4-18] Respect<br>• Professionals who demonstrate respect:<br>    ▪ Honor cultural diversity<br>    ▪ Affirm strengths<br>    ▪ Treat students and families with dignity | |
| [Slide 4-19] Commitment<br>• A committed professional will:<br>    ▪ Be available and accessible<br>    ▪ Go "above and beyond"<br>    ▪ Be sensitive to emotional needs | |
| [Slide 4-20] Equity<br>• Professionals who seek equality in partnerships:<br>    ▪ Share power<br>    ▪ Foster empowerment<br>    ▪ Provide options | |

| | |
|---|---|
| [Slide 4-21] Advocacy<br>• To be an effective advocate, professionals will:<br>    ▪ Seek win-win solutions<br>    ▪ Use skilled dialogue<br>    ▪ Prevent problems<br>    ▪ Keep one's conscience primed<br>    ▪ Pinpoint and document challenges<br>    ▪ Form alliances | |
| [Slide 4-22] Trust<br>• Four practices associated with being a trusted partner:<br>    ▪ Be reliable<br>    ▪ Use sound judgment<br>    ▪ Maintain confidentiality<br>    ▪ Trust yourself | |
| [Slide 4-23] Looking to Sean's Future<br>• Sean's life can be described as having five circles: Circle of Tears, Circle of Triumph, Circle of Transition Terror, his adult life, and his life as a man at the edges of life<br>• Sean's greatest security for his future depends on the willingness of his family and various professionals to be committed partners | |

## Activities: Applying Your Learning

Just as the textbook described Universal Design for Learning as the way for you to teach children, the principles work well for adult learners too. Rather than just taking notes, taking quizzes, and writing essays, the following activities will help you to learn the material on a deeper level and remember it better.

1. Self-Determination. Self-determination is a very important topic concerning individuals with disabilities. One of the errors teachers make is not being aware of the age appropriateness of certain decisions. One way to remember what is age appropriate is to remember when you became "self-determined" yourself. For this exercise, make a timeline of your own life for the following activities, and place them on the timeline on the following page.

When is the first time you were able to . . . ?

    a. Choose which food to eat first
    b. Choose which toys to play with
    c. Choose your bedtime
    d. Get dressed yourself
    e. Choose what clothes to wear
    f. Tie your shoes
    g. Choose what extracurricular hobby/activity you like to do
    h. Go on a sleepover
    i. Baby-sit another person
    j. Drive a car
    k. Have a bank account of your own
    l. Call up friends on the phone
    m. Choose who to be friends with

**AGES**

```
0         5         10         15        20
<------------------------------------------------>
```

What would it feel like if you had only accomplished half of the items on the list? Or none of them? How restricted would your life be? Why is it important to give individuals with disabilities the ability to determine their own lives?

2. Partnerships with families. Partnerships with families are imperative when planning for the success of children with disabilities. Give one specific example of how you can accomplish each of the major principles of building successful partnerships with the families of the students in your classroom. Make sure your examples address most of the bulleted points.

| Principle | How will you accomplish this successfully? |
|---|---|
| Communication<br><br>• Be friendly<br>• Listen<br>• Be clear<br>• Be honest<br>• Provide and coordinate information | |
| Personal Competence<br><br>• Providing a quality education<br>• Continuing to learn<br>• Setting high expectations | |
| Respect<br><br>• Honor cultural diversity<br>• Affirm strengths<br>• Treat students and families with dignity | |
| Commitment<br><br>• Be available and accessible<br>• Go above and beyond<br>• Be sensitive to emotional needs | |
| Equality<br><br>• Share power<br>• Foster empowerment<br>• Provide options | |

| | |
|---|---|
| Advocacy<br><br>   • Seek win-win solutions<br>   • Prevent problems<br>   • Keep your conscience primed<br>   • Pinpoint and document problems<br>   • Form alliances | |
| Trust<br><br>   • Being reliable<br>   • Using sound judgment<br>   • Maintaining confidentiality<br>   • Trusting yourself | |

3. Other interactive activities are available at the Companion Website found at http://www.prenhall.com/turnbull. Special Connections has an excellent case study called, "Parents as Partners." Here you can experience what it is like to collaborate with a parent who has concerns about the method of instruction a teacher has chosen for his or her child.

4. Do not forget the DVD cases packaged with your textbook. There you can see video clips of the individuals discussed in the book.

Use your *Real Lives & Exceptionalities* DVD to see Barbara discussing her "forever family" (Clip 4). What are the joys and challenges Barbara faces with Star?

Using your *Real Lives & Exceptionalities* DVD, view clips of each student's family highlighted in orange. How are the families different? How are they similar?

To see an example of a sibling talking about her relationship with her brother Ryan, go to the *Real Lives & Exceptionalities* DVD and view Clip 5 under "Meet Ryan."

To meet a university professor who has an exceptionality and who went through the educational system before PL 94-142, visit "Maxine" (Clip 3) under "Beyond School" on the *Real Lives & Exceptionalities* DVD.

*The questions that correspond to the DVD case studies are on the DVD, but they are also found in the back of this Student Study Guide. This will allow you to see the questions ahead of time. You are also welcome to write notes or answer the questions before typing them on the DVD.*

## Practice Quiz: Assessing Your Knowledge

Below are some questions to help you review the content in the chapter. Answers to the questions are provided for you at the end of the Student Study Guide. Circle the correct answer for each question.

1. A family is defined as:       PRAXIS 3           CEC 3
    A. Two or more people who carry out the functions of caring for each other
    B. Two or more persons who are related
    C. Two or more persons who are not related to each other
    D. None of the above

2. Thirty-five percent of students with disabilities live in households with annual incomes of:
          PRAXIS 3           CEC 3
    A. $35,000–$40,000
    B. $25,000–$35,000
    C. Less than $25,000
    D. Over $50,000

3. Which group is 2.5 times more likely to experience poverty?     PRAXIS 3      CEC 3
    A. Native Americans
    B. African Americans
    C. Hispanics
    D. Asian Americans

4. Students with disabilities also have a higher percentage of _____ as compared to youth without disabilities.
          PRAXIS 3          CEC 3
    A. Households with no biological parent
    B. Single-parent households
    C. Number of children in the household
    D. All of the above

5. One educational impact of poverty is:    PRAXIS 3         CEC 10
    A. Parental involvement
    B. More tutoring in schools
    C. Lack of parental involvement
    D. Lack of educational resources

6. What is the percentage of parents who believe that the school is doing a poor job of giving the help that their child needs?       PRAXIS 3         CEC 10
    A. 90%
    B. 75%
    C. 33%
    D. 10%

7. Parents' advocacy resulted in Congress enacting:     PRAXIS 2       CEC 10
    A. *Brown v. Board of Education*
    B. *Mills v. DC Board of Education*
    C. *Individuals with Disabilities Education Act*
    D. *Cedar Rapids v. Garrott F.*

8. Which of the following groups of parents are more likely to consider legal action against a school system?
          PRAXIS 3         CEC 10
    A. Parents of children with severe disabilities
    B. Parents of children with mild disabilities
    C. Parents of children with physical disabilities
    D. All groups are equally likely to consider legal action

9. In the educational system, parents want to be:     PRAXIS 3          CEC 10
   A. Adversaries
   B. Partners
   C. Advocates
   D. None of the above

10. A major complaint by parents is:     PRAXIS 3          CEC 10
    A. The lack of training of the professionals
    B. The lack of teachers on waivers
    C. The lack of student restraints
    D. The lack of cooperation on the part of the administrators

11. What type of partnership should professionals establish with parents?     PRAXIS 3     CEC 10
    A. Trusting
    B. Advocating
    C. Educational
    D. Valued

12. An important partnership principle is:     PRAXIS 3          CEC 10
    A. Advocacy
    B. Licensure
    C. Communication
    D. Both A and C

13. One way professionals can show respect for parents is to:     PRAXIS 3          CEC 10
    A. Affirm strengths
    B. Honor cultural diversity
    C. Treat students and families with dignity
    D. All of the above

14. One way for professionals to advocate effectively is to:     PRAXIS 3          CEC 10
    A. Develop a win-win situation
    B. Develop a win-lose situation
    C. Pinpoint and document solutions
    D. All of the above

15. Collaboration benefits which of the following groups:     PRAXIS 2          CEC 10
    A. Parents
    B. Students
    C. Professionals
    D. All of the above

Now that you have completed your chapter study, go back to the chapter objectives and see if you have truly met them. You may want to write out your responses to the chapter objectives so that you can check your understanding against the chapter outline or the text.

# Chapter 5: Understanding Students with Learning Disabilities

## Objectives: Guiding Your Chapter Reading

The content in this chapter is presented to help you achieve the following objectives. Once you complete your study of the chapter, see if you can do what the objectives describe. If not, you may need to do some more reviewing of the chapter and your class notes.

- Define and identify the characteristics of students with learning disabilities
- Recall the major causes of learning disabilities
- Explain the assessment and evaluation practices for students with learning disabilities
- Identify the major issues impacting students with learning disabilities
- Describe successful instructional practices and accommodations for students with learning disabilities

## Standards Matrices: Relating Content to Professional Standards

The matrices, or charts, below help you see how the professional standards from the Council for Exceptional Children (CEC) and PRAXIS™ apply to the content in this chapter. In addition, you can refer to the margin notes throughout the chapter and the activities at the end of each chapter to make sure you understand how these standards apply to the content in the field of special education. These standards are important for you to know because they provide the basis for the professional teacher certification examinations and content covered in these exams.

| CEC Standards | Chapter Topics |
|---|---|
| 1 | <ul><li>IDEA</li><li>Defining learning disabilities</li><li>Identification</li><li>Discrepancy standard for learning disabilities</li><li>Appropriate education</li></ul> |
| 2 | <ul><li>Case Study</li><li>Characteristics of learning disabilities</li><li>Characteristics of learning disabilities as they relate to academic achievement</li><li>Characteristics of learning disabilities as they relate to social, emotional, and behavioral characteristics</li><li>Causes of learning disabilities</li></ul> |
| 3 | <ul><li>Characteristics of learning disabilities as they relate to academic achievement</li><li>Universal design</li><li>Differentiated instruction</li><li>Learning strategies</li><li>Accommodations</li></ul> |
| 4 | <ul><li>Response to intervention model</li><li>Curriculum mapping</li><li>Differentiated instruction</li><li>Learning strategies</li><li>Universal design for learning as it relates to advanced organizers</li></ul> |
| 5 | <ul><li>Student involvement in educational planning</li><li>Curriculum mapping</li><li>Transition</li><li>Early intervention</li><li>Inclusion</li></ul> |
| 6 | <ul><li>Early intervention</li></ul> |
| 7 | <ul><li>Partnering for special education services</li><li>Early intervention</li><li>Transition</li></ul> |

| CEC Standards | Chapter Topics |
|---|---|
| 8 | <ul><li>Evaluation and assessment of learning disabilities</li><li>Nondiscriminatory evaluation</li><li>Discrepancy model</li><li>Intelligence tests</li><li>Response to intervention model</li><li>Specially designed instruction and services</li><li>Measuring student progress</li></ul> |
| 9 | <ul><li>Curriculum mapping</li></ul> |
| 10 | <ul><li>Case Study</li><li>Partnering for special education services</li><li>Curriculum mapping</li><li>Transition</li></ul> |

| PRAXIS™ Standards | Chapter Topics |
|---|---|
| 1 | <ul><li>Case Study</li><li>Identification</li><li>Characteristics of learning disabilities</li><li>Causes of learning disabilities</li></ul> |
| 2 | <ul><li>IDEA</li><li>Defining learning disabilities</li><li>Appropriate education</li></ul> |
| 3 | <ul><li>Characteristics of learning disabilities as they relate to academic achievement</li><li>Partnering for special education services</li><li>Curriculum mapping</li><li>Early intervention</li><li>Inclusion</li><li>Transition</li><li>Differentiated instruction</li><li>Learning strategies</li><li>Universal design for learning as it relates to advanced organizers</li><li>Evaluation and assessment of learning disabilities</li><li>Nondiscriminatory evaluation</li><li>Discrepancy model</li><li>Intelligence tests</li><li>Response to intervention model</li><li>Specially designed instruction and services</li><li>Measuring student progress</li></ul> |

## Checking for Understanding: Key Terms

To check that you understand the basic terms and vocabulary in the chapter, use the space provided to write the definitions or descriptions in your own words. Then, check the chapter to see how accurate your definition is, making sure you understand the context, or situation, in which the word is used. Reviewing these terms will help you better understand the concepts that support the content in this chapter.

| Term | Definition/Description | (✓) |
|---|---|---|
| differentiated instruction | | |
| specific learning disability | | |
| inclusionary standard | | |
| exclusionary standard | | |
| dyslexia | | |
| dysgraphia | | |
| dyscalculia | | |
| procedural problems | | |
| semantic memory problems | | |
| visual-spatial problems | | |
| mnemonics | | |

| | | |
|---|---|---|
| teratagens | | |
| discrepancy model | | |
| norm-referenced | | |
| standard deviation | | |
| mean | | |
| aptitude-achievement | | |
| intracognitive | | |
| intra-achievement | | |
| IQ-achievement discrepancy | | |
| response to intervention | | |
| phonological processing | | |
| learning strategies | | |
| curriculum-based measurement (CBM) | | |

## Chapter Outline: Taking Chapter Notes

The following outline is taken from the PowerPoint slides or overheads that your professor uses in class for this chapter. In the slides, there are several embedded links to more information for this chapter. Please go to the Companion Website at http://www.prenhall.com/turnbull to access them easily.

If you take your Student Study Guide to class, you can use this outline for taking notes on the chapter or for review. It will also allow you to listen to lectures and participate in class discussions without having to copy down all the PowerPoint information.

The notes below are set up for recording information from the chapter in a particular way—an adapted Cornell method of taking notes. In this adapted Cornell method, you underline, or highlight, information presented to you. In addition to highlighting, you can write information or explanations on the left-hand side of the table. Soon after the class presentation or reading the chapter, rewrite the notes from the left-hand side in your own words, using key terms and phrases. To study for quizzes or exams, you can cover up the left-hand side and use the right-hand side of the table to cue yourself about the information.

You also may just jot notes on the right-hand side to help you. Since this outline reduces the chapter for you, it will be a useful study aid. The summary at the end of the chapter is another useful resource to use for review.

| Chapter 5<br>Understanding Students with Learning Disabilities | NOTES |
| --- | --- |
| [Slide 5-1] Chapter 5 Objectives: At the end of this chapter you should be able to:<br>• Define and identify the characteristics of students with learning disabilities<br>• Recall the major causes of learning disabilities<br>• Explain the assessment and evaluation practices for students with learning disabilities<br>• Identify the major issues impacting students with learning disabilities<br>• Describe successful instructional practices and accommodations for students with learning disabilities | |
| [Slide 5-2] Who Is Lauren Marsh?<br>• Lauren is an eighth-grade student; she is considered a "peacemaker."<br>• She is included in the general education classroom, leaving only once a week to receive special training in reading strategies.<br>• Lauren receives a great deal of help from her teacher, Sherry Eichinger.<br>• Sherry acts as a collaborator, working with the IEP team, as well as helping Lauren and other students with disabilities work in the general education classroom.<br>• Collaborative efforts from Lauren's dad, mother, and teacher have helped Lauren gain ability and confidence.<br>• Sherry is also taking steps to teach Lauren self-advocacy so that she can become a self-determined adult. | |

| | |
|---|---|
| [Slide 5-3] Defining Learning Disabilities<br>• IDEA definition<br>    ▪ Specific learning disability<br>    ▪ Basic psychological processes<br>• Criteria for classification<br>    ▪ Inclusionary standard<br>    ▪ Exclusionary standard | |
| [Slide 5-4] Prevalence of Learning Disabilities<br>• Most prevalent of all disabilities<br>• Recent trends and increases<br>• Since 1975, numbers have nearly tripled<br>• Dramatic increase over all ethnic groups except Asian/Pacific Islander students<br>• More from lower socioeconomic backgrounds<br>• Many more boys than girls | |
| [Slide 5-5] Describing the Characteristics<br>•    Academic Achievement Characteristics<br>    ▪ Reading<br>        • Dyslexia<br>    ▪ Written Language<br>        • Dysgraphia<br>    ▪ Mathematics<br>        • Dyscalculia<br>    ▪ Memory<br>    ▪ Metacognition<br>        • Mnemonics<br>• Social, Emotional and Behavioral Characteristics<br>    ▪ Interpersonal Skills<br>    ▪ Self-Concept<br>    ▪ Impact of Label | |
| [Slide 5-6] Determining the Causes<br>• Neurological mechanisms<br>• Brain abnormalities found<br>• Genetics<br>• Strong evidence<br>• Environmental causes<br>    ▪ Teratogens | |
| [Slide 5-7] Nondiscriminatory Evaluation Process<br>(See Figure 5–2) | |
| [Slide 5-8] The Discrepancy Model<br>• Intelligence Tests<br>    ▪ Bell curve (See Figure 5–3)<br>    ▪ WISC-III<br>• Achievement Tests<br>    ▪ WIAT-II<br>• The discrepancy model compared two norm-referenced test scores:<br>    ▪ Aptitude-achievement<br>    ▪ Intracognitive<br>    ▪ Intra-achievement<br>• States each had different criteria<br>• Criticisms of the IQ-achievement discrepancy | |

| | |
|---|---|
| [Slide 5-9] Response-to-Intervention Process<br>• Start with "generally effective" instruction<br>• Monitor student's progress<br>• If unsuccessful—intervene<br>• More explicit, intensive, and/or supportive instruction<br>    ▪ Monitor student's progress again<br>    ▪ If unsuccessful—child may either qualify for special education or for special education evaluation | |
| [Slide 5-10] Response-to-Intervention Process<br>• Five potential benefits:<br>    ▪ Earlier intervention and support to child<br>    ▪ Differentiates students with LD from students needing remediation<br>    ▪ No labels needed to receive services<br>    ▪ Provides support to other students who need help but who are not eligible<br>    ▪ No IQ testing needed for eligibility | |
| [Slide 5-11] Partnering for Special Education and Related Services<br>• Include the child with a disability in planning<br>• Student involvement can take many different forms:<br>    ▪ Self-directed IEP<br>    ▪ Self-Advocacy Strategy<br>    ▪ Self-Determined Learning Model of Instruction | |
| [Slide 5-12] Determining Supplementary Aids and Services<br>• Curriculum Mapping<br>    ▪ Educators collect information about each teacher's curriculum, using the school calendar as an organizer<br>    ▪ They then can determine what they are teaching<br>    ▪ Can identify where students can receive instruction on content from the general curriculum | |
| [Slide 5-13] Planning for Universal Design for Learning<br>• Advanced organizers<br>• Graphic organizers<br>• How do they help students?<br>• What are some examples?<br>    ▪ lesson organizers<br>    ▪ chapter survey routines<br>    ▪ unit organizers<br>    ▪ course organizers | |

| | |
|---|---|
| [Slide 5-14] Planning for Other Educational Needs<br>• Transition Success Skills for College (in priority order)<br>    ▪ Understanding their disability<br>    ▪ Understanding their strengths and limitations<br>    ▪ Learning to succeed despite their disability and what accommodations facilitate learning<br>    ▪ Setting goals and learning how to access resources<br>    ▪ Problem solving skills<br>    ▪ Self-management skills<br>    ▪ Forming relationships with university personnel, peers, and mentors | |
| [Slide 5-15] Early Childhood Students<br>• Embedded Learning Opportunities (ELO)<br>    ▪ Practiced in context of daily activities<br>    ▪ Can be used in inclusive environments<br>    ▪ Capitalizes on child's interest and motivation<br>    ▪ Is available to parents, teachers, therapists, and peers<br>    ▪ Is compatible with a wide range of curricular models | |
| [Slide 5-16] Elementary and Middle School Students<br>• Differentiated Instruction<br>    ▪ Provide visual or graphic organizer<br>    ▪ Incorporate models, demonstrations, or role play<br>    ▪ Using teacher presentation cues to emphasize key points<br>    ▪ Scaffolding key concepts<br>    ▪ Getting students actively involved in the learning process using every-pupil response techniques or manipulatives | |
| [Slide 5-17] Secondary and Transition Students<br>• Learning Strategies<br>    ▪ Assess how well a student can perform the skill<br>    ▪ Point out the benefit of using learning strategies<br>    ▪ Explain specifically what a student will be able to accomplish once he or she knows the skill<br>    ▪ Types of Learning Strategies<br>• Acquiring information<br>• Storing information and remembering<br>• Examples<br>    ▪ Center for Research on Learning<br>    ▪ The Learning ToolBox | |
| [Slide 5-18] Educational Placement (See Figure 5–5) | |

| | |
|---|---|
| [Slide 5-19] Measuring Students' Progress<br>• Curriculum-Based Assessment<br>    ▪ Chart a student's progress in the general curriculum<br>    ▪ Brief timed samples or probes of academic material directly from curriculum<br>    ▪ Probes given under standardized conditions<br>    ▪ Scored on speed or fluency or accuracy<br>    ▪ Can be given repeatedly since it is quick and easy to score<br>• Progress for other educational needs such as social skills are measured using rating scales or sociometrics | |
| [Slide 5-20] Making Accommodations for Assessment<br>• Concerns with testing accommodations<br>• Examples of testing accommodations:<br>    ▪ Reader<br>    ▪ Extended time<br>    ▪ Use of computers for test administration<br>    ▪ Calculators | |
| [Slide 5-21] Looking to Lauren's Future<br>• Planning Lauren's transition from high school to community college<br>• Supporting Lauren's success in interpersonal skills to professional and volunteer activities<br>• Including Lauren and her parents as part of the collaborative team | |

## Activities: Applying Your Learning

Just as the textbook described Universal Design for Learning as the way for you to teach children, the principles work well for adult learners too. Rather than just taking notes, taking quizzes, and writing essays, the following activities will help you to learn the material on a deeper level and remember it better.

1. Graphic Organizers. Graphic organizers are one type of advanced organizer that assists all learners, including those with learning disabilities. Let's make a classic graphic organizer called a "mind map," "web," or "spider chart." Start by drawing a circle in the center and put the main topic in the center (already provided for you below). Off the center are subconcepts and then details describing the subconcepts. This graphic organizer about graphic organizers has already been started for you. To get the complete information about graphic organizers so you can complete it, go to http://www.cast.org/publications/ncac/ncac_go.html.

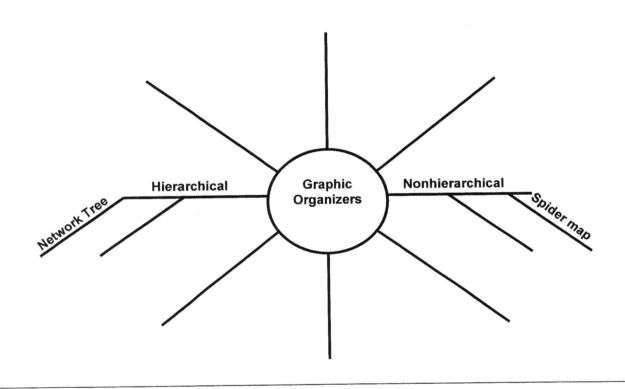

2. Response to Intervention. Response to intervention is a big change from the discrepancy model. Give the pros and cons of each model in the diagram below to help your understanding.

| Discrepancy Model Pros | Response to Intervention Pros |
|---|---|
| | |
| **Discrepancy Model Cons** | **Response to Intervention Cons** |
| | |

3. Other interactive activities are available at the Companion Website found at http://www.prenhall.com/turnbull. For you to examine exactly what it feels like to have a learning disability, make sure to do the simulations at "Misunderstood Minds" and view the "FAT City" video clip.

4. Do not forget the DVD cases packaged with your textbook. There you can see video clips of the individuals discussed in the book.

View Clip 5 in "Meet Heather" on the *Real Lives & Exceptionalities* DVD and compare it to what you read about Lauren in this chapter. How are Lauren and Heather's learning disabilities different? How are they similar?

Use your *Real Lives & Exceptionalities* DVD to meet Ms. Guinn, a fifth-grade teacher discussing differentiated instruction. Click on "Meet Heather," and select "Accommodations" (Clip 2). Do you believe differentiated instruction is a good solution for Heather? Would it work for Lauren?

*The questions that correspond to the DVD case studies are on the DVD, but they are also found in the back of this Student Study Guide. This will allow you to see the questions ahead of time. You are also welcome to write notes or answer the questions before typing them on the DVD.*

## Practice Quiz: Assessing Your Knowledge

Below are some questions to help you review the content in the chapter. Answers to the questions are provided for you at the end of the Student Study Guide. Circle the correct answer for each question.

1. In which year did Sam Kirk coin the term "learning disabilities"?   PRAXIS 1        CEC 1
    A. 1940
    B. 1963
    C. 1975
    D. 1990

2. Karen meets the exclusionary criteria for learning disabilities. What does this mean? PRAXIS 1        CEC 1
    A. She has a severe discrepancy between perceived potential and actual achievement.
    B. She manifests a demonstrated need for special education.
    C. Her learning issues are not the primary result of other disabilities like mental retardation, sensory impairments, or emotional disabilities.
    D. She has never been retained in school or received special education prior to this time so she does not have a learning disability.

3. What is the formula for determining IQ?        PRAXIS 1                CEC 8
    A.  $CA \div MA \times 100$
    B.  $MA \div CA \times 100$
    C.  $CA \div 100 \times MA$
    D.  $MA \div 100 \times CA$

4. Jose's IQ fell at the 50th percentile. According to the bell curve, approximately what was Jose's IQ score?
        PRAXIS 1                CEC 8
    A.  His IQ score was about 50
    B.  His IQ score was about 100
    C.  His IQ score was about 150
    D.  Cannot tell given this information

5. Kaiekka has difficulty with phonological awareness. Which statement below best describes her difficulty?
        PRAXIS 1                CEC 8
    A.  She has difficulty remembering oral directions.
    B.  She has difficulty expressing herself orally.
    C.  She has difficulty segmenting sounds in words.
    D.  She has difficulty with reversing letters and numbers.

6. Which term below refers to a disability in the area of mathematics?        PRAXIS 1        CEC 8
    A.  Dyslexia
    B.  Dysgraphia
    C.  Dyscalculia
    D.  Dysnomia

7. Roberta makes acronyms for lists to remember items for a test. Which strategy is Roberta using?
        PRAXIS 3                CEC 8
    A.  Learned helplessness
    B.  Mnemonics
    C.  Phonological awareness
    D.  Cognitive engagement

8. What is happening with a student who is dependent upon others rather than developing his or her own metacognitive skills?    PRAXIS 3            CEC3
    A. Learned helplessness
    B. Outer directedness
    C. Self-determination
    D. Both A and B

9. Which academic skill area affects the majority of students with learning disabilities? PRAXIS 3        CEC 3
    A. Reading
    B. Written language
    C. Mathematics
    D. Science

10. Which statement describes Direct Instruction?    PRAXIS 3                CEC 7
    A. It is an approach that emphasizes discovery learning in the basic skill areas and some content areas.
    B. It is an approach that emphasizes developmentally appropriate activities such as using manipulatives for teaching math, science, and social studies.
    C. It is an approach that emphasizes using graphic organizers for teaching content area information.
    D. It is an approach that emphasizes teaching skills in a particular order with scripted teacher lessons.

11. What are the six defining characteristics of learning disabilities?    PRAXIS 1            CEC 2
    A. Reading, spelling, math, attention, memory, and interpersonal skills
    B. Reading, written language, math, memory, behavior, and attention
    C. Reading, written language, science, social studies, attention, and memory
    D. Reading, written language, math, attention, memory, and metacognition

12. What are some uses of the results from curriculum based measurement?    PRAXIS 3        CEC 8
    A. CBM results help in developing a student's IEP
    B. CBM results help in monitoring the student's progress
    C. CBM results help in determining instructional effectiveness
    D. All of the above

13. Students write words that are dictated to them for a specified time and the correct letter sequences are counted. This is known as:    PRAXIS 3                CEC 8
    A. Curriculum-based assessment
    B. Curriculum-based measurement
    C. Direct Instruction
    D. KTEA

14. Why do teachers use differentiated instruction in their classrooms?        PRAXIS 3        CEC 4
    A. To promote active participation
    B. To directly instruct students using a scripted lesson
    C. To promote progress through the general curriculum
    D. Both A and C

15. Students learning how to develop their own learning strategies is known as:        PRAXIS 3        CEC 4
    A. Cognitive
    B. Metacognition
    C. Reading skills
    D. Cognition

Now that you have completed your chapter study, go back to the chapter objectives and see if you have truly met them. You may want to write out your responses to the chapter objectives so that you can check your understanding against the chapter outline or the text.

# Chapter 6: Understanding Students with Communication Disorders

## Objectives: Guiding Your Chapter Reading

The content in this chapter is presented to help you achieve the following objectives. Once you complete your study of the chapter, see if you can do what the objectives describe. If not, you may need to do some more reviewing of the chapter and your class notes.

- Define and identify the characteristics of students with communication disorders
- Recall the major causes of communication disorders
- Explain the assessment and evaluation practices for students with communication disorders
- Identify the major issues impacting students with communication disorders
- Describe successful instructional practices and accommodations for students with communication disorders

## Standards Matrices: Relating Content to Professional Standards

The matrices, or charts, below help you see how the professional standards from the Council for Exceptional Children (CEC) and PRAXIS™ apply to the content in this chapter. In addition, you can refer to the margin notes throughout the chapter and the activities at the end of each chapter to make sure you understand how these standards apply to the content in the field of special education. These standards are important for you to know because they provide the basis for the professional teacher certification examinations and content covered in these exams.

| CEC Standards | Chapter Topics |
|---|---|
| 1 | <ul><li>IDEA</li><li>Defining communication disorders as they relate to speech and language</li><li>Social interaction theories</li></ul> |
| 2 | <ul><li>Case study</li><li>Characteristics of speech and language disabilities</li><li>Articulation disorders</li><li>Voice disorders</li><li>Fluency disorders</li><li>Language impairments as they relate to phonology, morphology, syntax, and pragmatics</li><li>Causes of communication disorders</li></ul> |
| 3 | <ul><li>Universal design for learning</li><li>Accommodations</li></ul> |
| 4 | <ul><li>Activity clusters</li><li>Universal design for learning</li><li>Effective instructional strategies</li></ul> |
| 5 | <ul><li>Educational needs</li><li>Inclusion</li></ul> |
| 6 | <ul><li>Cultural diversity as it relates to language and speech</li><li>Interventions</li><li>Augmentative and alternative communication</li></ul> |
| 7 | <ul><li>Activity clusters</li><li>Universal design for learning</li><li>Effective instructional strategies</li></ul> |
| 8 | <ul><li>Evaluation and assessment</li><li>Multicultural considerations</li><li>Curriculum-based assessment</li><li>Measuring student progress in the general education curriculum</li></ul> |
| 9 | <ul><li>Characteristics of speech and language disabilities</li></ul> |
| 10 | <ul><li>Partnering for special education services</li><li>Activity clusters</li></ul> |

| PRAXIS™ Standards | Chapter Topics |
|---|---|
| 1 | • Case Study<br>• Characteristics of speech and language disabilities<br>• Articulation disorders<br>• Voice disorders<br>• Fluency disorders<br>• Language impairments as they relate to phonology, morphology, syntax, and pragmatics<br>• Causes of communication disorders |
| 2 | • IDEA<br>• Defining communication disorders as they relate to speech and language |
| 3 | • Activity clusters<br>• Universal design for learning<br>• Effective instructional strategies<br>• Activity clusters<br>• Educational needs<br>• Inclusion<br>• Cultural diversity as it relates to language and speech<br>• Interventions<br>• Augmentative and alternative communication<br>• Evaluation and assessment<br>• Multicultural considerations<br>• Curriculum-based assessment<br>• Measuring student progress in the general education curriculum<br>• Partnering for special education services<br>• Transition |

## Checking for Understanding: Key Terms

To check that you understand the basic terms and vocabulary in the chapter, use the space provided to write the definitions or descriptions in your own words. Then, check the chapter to see how accurate your definition is, making sure you understand the context, or situation, in which the word is used. Reviewing these terms will help you better understand the concepts that support the content in this chapter.

| Term | Definition/Description | (✓) |
|---|---|---|
| speech disorder | | |
| language disorder | | |
| receptive language disorder | | |

| | | |
|---|---|---|
| expressive language disorder | | |
| cleft palate or lip | | |
| dialect | | |
| speech | | |
| language | | |
| phonemes | | |
| morphemes | | |
| articulation | | |
| substitutions | | |
| omissions | | |
| additions | | |
| distortions | | |
| apraxia | | |

| | | |
|---|---|---|
| pitch | | |
| duration | | |
| resonance | | |
| hyponasality | | |
| hypernasality | | |
| fluency | | |
| specific language impairment | | |
| organic disorders | | |
| functional disorders | | |
| congenital disorder | | |
| acquired disorder | | |
| oral motor exam | | |
| bilingual | | |

| | | |
|---|---|---|
| bidialectal<br>System for Augmenting<br>Language (SAL) | | |
| **Additional Terms** | | |
| phonology | | |
| morphology | | |
| syntax | | |
| semantics | | |
| pragmatics | | |
| social interaction theories | | |
| augmentative and alternative<br>communication (AAC) | | |

## Chapter Outline: Taking Chapter Notes

The following outline is taken from the PowerPoint slides or overheads that your professor uses in class for this chapter. In the slides, there are several embedded links to more information for this chapter. Please go to the Companion Website at http://www.prenhall.com/turnbull to access them easily.

If you take your Student Study Guide to class, you can use this outline for taking notes on the chapter or for review. It will also allow you to listen to lectures and participate in class discussions without having to copy down all the PowerPoint information.

The notes below are set up for recording information from the chapter in a particular way—an adapted Cornell method of taking notes. In this adapted Cornell method, you underline, or highlight, information presented to you. In addition to highlighting, you can write information or explanations on the left-hand side of the table. Soon after the class presentation or reading the chapter, rewrite the notes from the left-hand side in your own words, using key terms and phrases. To study for quizzes or exams, you can cover up the left-hand side and use the right-hand side of the table to cue yourself about the information.

You also may just jot notes on the right-hand side to help you. Since this outline reduces the chapter for you, it will be a useful study aid. The summary at the end of the chapter is another useful resource to use for review.

| Chapter 6 Understanding Students with Communication Disorders | NOTES |
|---|---|
| [Slide 6-1] Chapter 6 Objectives: At the end of this chapter, you should be able to:<br><br>• Define and identify the characteristics of students with communication disorders<br>• Recall the major causes of communication disorders<br>• Explain the assessment and evaluation practices for students with communication disorders<br>• Identify the major issues impacting students with communication disorders<br>• Describe successful instructional practices and accommodations for students with communication disorders | |
| [Slide 6-2] Who Is George Wedge?<br><br>• George is a 7-year-old boy with a communication disorder since birth due to a congenital brain malformation.<br>• As soon as he was born, he was enrolled in an early intervention program.<br>• He was in such programs up until his enrollment in his local kindergarten classroom.<br>• George has learned ASL and finger spelling, as well as how to use an assistive technology device.<br>• A strong collaborative team has worked to prepare for George's next steps and assure he gets all the services he needs. | |
| [Slide 6-3] Defining Communication Disorders<br><br>• Communication: Entails receiving, understanding, and expressing information, feelings, and ideas<br>• Speech disorder: Refers to difficulty in producing sounds<br>• Language disorder: Refers to difficulty in receiving, understanding, and formulating ideas and information<br>• Two forms of language: Expressive and Receptive<br>• Cultural diversity<br>    • Difference does not always mean disorder.<br>    • Dialects are various forms of language. | |

| | |
|---|---|
| [Slide 6-4] Prevalence of Communication Disorders<br>• Of all students receiving special education services, about 18.8% receive speech and language services.<br>• 55% of children 3–5 served under IDEA have speech-language disorders<br>• Most are in the general education classroom | |
| [Slide 6-5] Typical Development<br>• Speech: Oral expression of language<br>• Language: Structured, shared, rule-governed, symbolic system for communicating<br>• Phonology (phonemes): Sound system, (sound unit)<br>• Morphology (morphemes): Word forms (meaning unit)<br>• Syntax: Word order and sentence structure<br>• Semantics: Word and sentence meanings<br>• Pragmatics: Use of communication contexts<br>• Social interaction theories: Communication skills through social interactions | |
| [Slide 6-6] Speech Disorders<br>• Articulation: Production of individual or sequenced sounds<br>  ▪ Substitutions, Omissions, Additions, Distortions<br>• Apraxia of speech: Motor speech disorder affecting the planning of speech<br>• Voice disorders: Pitch, Duration, Intensity, Resonance<br>  ▪ Hyponasality, Hypernasality<br>• Fluency disorders: Interruptions in the flow of speaking<br>  ▪ Stuttering | |
| [Slide 6-7] Language Impairments<br>• Language disorders may be receptive, expressive, or both.<br>• Language disorders may be related to another disability or may be a specific language impairment. | |
| [Slide 6-8] Language Impairments<br>• Phonological disorders: Difficulty in discriminating differences in speech sounds or sound segments<br>• Morphological difficulties: Problem using the structure of words to get or give information<br>• Syntactical errors: Problems involving word order, incorrect structure, misuse of negatives, or omitting structures<br>• Semantic disorders: Problems using words singly or together in sentences<br>• Pragmatic disorders: Problems in the social use of language | |

| | |
|---|---|
| [Slide 6-9] Determining the Causes<br>• Organic: Caused by an identifiable problem in the neuromuscular mechanism<br>• Functional: Those with no identifiable origin<br>• Congenital: Present at birth<br>• Acquired: Occurs well after birth | |
| [Slide 6-10] Nondiscriminatory Evaluation Process (See Figure 6–3) | |
| [Slide 6-11] Determining the Presence<br>• Speech assessment<br>  ▪ Articulation and apraxia<br>  ▪ Voice<br>  ▪ Fluency<br>• Language Assessments<br>• Multicultural considerations<br>  ▪ Bilingual<br>  ▪ Bidialectal | |
| [Slide 6-12] Partnering for Special Education and Related Services<br>• Collaboration<br>• Roles of speech-language pathologists<br>• Partnership Tips (p. 143)<br>  ▪ Consultation<br>  ▪ Supportive teaching<br>  ▪ Complementary teaching<br>  ▪ Include speech-language pathologist in curriculum planning and instructional opportunities | |
| [Slide 6-13] Determining Supplementary Aids and Services<br>• Augmentative and alternative communication (AAC) systems<br>  ▪ AAC systems are components that supplement the communication abilities of individuals<br>  ▪ May include an AAC device, which is a physical object that transmits or receives messages<br>  ▪ Communication books, communication/language boards, communication charts, mechanical or electronic voice output equipment, or computers<br>  ▪ An AAC device has two components: a symbol set and a means for selecting the symbols<br>  ▪ Devices can range from low tech, such as line-drawn pictures within a notebook or wallet, to high tech | |

| | |
|---|---|
| [Slide 6-14] Planning for Universal Design for Learning<br>• Vary the ways in which the teacher communicates<br>    ▪ Using audio and text formats<br>    ▪ Visual representations with verbal information<br>    ▪ Graphics, graphic organizers, and controlled vocabulary | |
| [Slide 6-15] Planning for Universal Design for Learning<br>• Vary the ways that students demonstrate their knowledge<br>    ▪ Asking a student to convert a written report to a PowerPoint presentation<br>    ▪ Supplementing a demonstration with visual supports<br>    ▪ Using a taped oral report<br>    ▪ Performing a skit solo or with others | |
| [Slide 6-16] Planning for Other Educational Needs<br>• Building Social Relationships<br>    ▪ May need to be taught specific social skills<br>    ▪ May need support to initiate and sustain interactions because of their limited expressive language<br>• Social Stories<br>    ▪ Describes social concepts, skills, or situations by providing information about the situation and people involved | |

| | |
|---|---|
| [Slide 6-17] Early Childhood Students<br>• Facilitative Language Strategies (Into Practice, p. 147)<br>    ▪ Focused contrast<br>    ▪ Modeling<br>    ▪ Events casts<br>    ▪ Open questions<br>    ▪ Expansions<br>    ▪ Recasts<br>    ▪ Redirects and prompted initiations | |
| [Slide 6-18] Elementary and Middle School Students<br>• Graphic Organizer Modifications<br>    ▪ Support transitions to reading and writing<br>    ▪ Use graphic organizers to develop literacy skills<br>        • Provide a visual representation in an organized framework<br>        • Can be hand-drawn or computer generated | |
| [Slide 6-19] Secondary and Transition Students<br>• AAC systems<br>    ▪ Include sign language; picture communication books, boards, or cards; and electronic communication devices<br>    ▪ Learning to use AAC systems takes a team effort<br>    ▪ AAC instructional strategies should focus on teaching communication rather than teaching the student to use AAC<br>    ▪ System for augmenting language (SAL) | |
| [Slide 6-20] Educational Placement (See Figure 6–5) | |
| [Slide 6-21] Measuring Students' Progress<br>• Progress in the general curriculum data-based performance modification procedure, usually curriculum-based assessments<br>• Teachers and SLPs reduce the discrepancy between the student's current communication skill level and the curriculum standard<br>• Other educational needs can be assessed through ecological inventories | |

| | |
|---|---|
| [Slide 6-22] Making Accommodations for Assessment<br>• Accommodations:<br>    ▪ No accommodations<br>    ▪ Additional time<br>    ▪ Access to a word processor/computer software<br>• Present information in a manner that assists the student's comprehension<br>• If the student has difficulty expressing herself, she may benefit from a format that does not require long verbal or written output<br>• Format should complement the student's most common means of expression | |
| [Slide 6-23] Looking to George's Future<br>▪ George's parents would like to see him eventually attend college.<br>▪ They want him to be self-determined and follow his own dreams.<br>▪ Communication will continue to be a focus for his educational participation, and technology may grow in importance. | |

## Activities: Applying Your Learning

Just as the textbook described Universal Design for Learning as the way for you to teach children, the principles work well for adult learners too. Rather than just taking notes, taking quizzes, and writing essays, the following activities will help you to learn the material on a deeper level and remember it better.

1. Text-to-Speech. Want to try out text-to-speech? Type something in the following demo and the computer will speak for you. You can also copy and paste larger amounts of text, up to 300 characters. Try out the different voices.

AT&T text-to-speech can be found at http://www.research.att.com/projects/tts/demo.html.

- How natural does the voice sound?


- Does it sound computerized or more natural than you thought?


- Did it make any errors?


- Even though this is not designed as an AAC device, if you needed to use a device like this to speak, how difficult would it be?

2. Receptive and Expressive Language. When do we use language in the classroom? Give specific examples of when students use receptive language and expressive language. Make sure you can generate at least 10 specific examples of each.

| Receptive Language Examples | Expressive Language Examples |
|---|---|
|  |  |

How difficult would it be for a student to function if he or she had deficits in receptive and/or expressive language and could not do the examples on your list?

3. Other interactive activities are available at the Companion Website found at http://www.prenhall.com/turnbull. There are several videos and examples of individuals using AAC and the considerations to examine when selecting AAC devices. Check out the video showing how a speech-language pathologist (SLP) and teacher collaborate in the classroom from Whole Schooling Consortium.

4. Do not forget the DVD cases packaged with your textbook. There you can see video clips of the individuals discussed in the book.

Use your *Real Lives & Exceptionalities* DVD to "Meet George." Use your *Real Lives & Exceptionalities* DVD to view the "Accommodation" (Clip 2) and "Collaboration" (Clips 3 and 5) videos.

How do George's teachers and family include George in daily activities?

*The questions that correspond to the DVD case studies are on the DVD, but they are also found in the back of this Student Study Guide. This will allow you to see the questions ahead of time. You are also welcome to write notes or answer the questions before typing them on the DVD.*

## Practice Quiz: Assessing Your Knowledge

Below are some questions to help you review the content in the chapter. Answers to the questions are provided for you at the end of the Student Study Guide. Circle the correct answer for each question.

1.  Which type of disorder refers to difficulty receiving, understanding, and formulating ideas and information?
    PRAXIS 1                CEC 2
    A.  Speech disorder
    B.  Language disorder
    C.  Apraxia
    D.  Articulation disorder

2.  Which list includes examples of fluency disorders?        PRAXIS 1                CEC 2
    A.  Substitutions, omissions, additions, and distortions
    B.  Pitch, duration, intensity, resonance, and vocal quality
    C.  Stuttering, rate, rhythm, repetitions
    D.  Substitutions, pitch, additions, stuttering

3.  Which type of language impairment describes Ronald, who makes comments unrelated to the conversation, uses inappropriate body language, and does not take turns in conversations?        PRAXIS 1                CEC 2
    A.  Phonology
    B.  Morphology
    C.  Syntax
    D.  Pragmatics

4.  Which type of language impairment describes Sue, who has difficulty discriminating speech sounds or segmenting sounds in words?        PRAXIS 1                CEC 2
    A.  Phonology
    B.  Morphology
    C.  Syntax
    D.  Pragmatics

5.  Using typical language developmental milestones, which of these would happen first?
    PRAXIS 1                CEC 2
    A.  The child recognizes and tells jokes
    B.  The child uses plurals
    C.  The child recounts events
    D.  The child points to pictures in a picture book

6.  Which of these sounds are typically mispronounced in people who lisp?        PRAXIS 1                CEC 2
    A.  S, t, r, n, and m
    B.  S, z, sh, and ch
    C.  P, m, h, n, and w
    D.  Zh, s, z, v, and th

7.  Which child below is bidialectal?        PRAXIS 1                CEC 2
    A.  Leo, who speaks English and Spanish
    B.  Craig, whose native language is Spanish
    C.  Marcus, who uses two variations of a language
    D.  Samantha, who uses two languages in two different environments

8.  Which of the following professionals completes most of the fluency assessments?        PRAXIS 3                CEC 8
    A.  General educator
    B.  Special educator
    C.  Speech-language pathologist
    D.  Occupational therapist

9.  Which of the following children is/are showing signs that are characteristic of apraxia?
    PRAXIS 1                CEC 2
    A.  Michael makes errors in the production of vowels.
    B.  Walter has an inconsistent pitch.
    C.  Riley has reappearing vocal nodules.
    D.  All of the above

10. Of all the students with a speech or language impairment being served, about what percentage also have a learning disability as a primary disability?     PRAXIS 3                CEC 2
    A.  100%
    B.  5%
    C.  10%
    D.  50%

11. Which term below refers to the condition associated with frequent repetition and/or prolongation of words or sounds?     PRAXIS 1                CEC 2
    A.  Lisp
    B.  Dialect
    C.  Stutter
    D.  Apraxia

12. The tool used that focuses on augmented input of language is known as:     PRAXIS 3          CEC 4
    A. SAL
    B. PAL
    C. LAS
    D. None of the above

13. A child who has difficulty receiving or understanding information has a(n):     PRAXIS 1          CEC 2
    A.  Expressive language disorder
    B.  Receptive language disorder
    C.  Speech disorder
    D.  Expressive and language disorder

14. When a group of individuals use a language variation that reflects a shared regional, social, or cultural/ethnic factor, this is known as:     PRAXIS 1                CEC 2
    A.  Accent
    B.  Dialect
    C.  Language
    D.  Speech

15. Which member of the team tries to reduce the discrepancy between the student's current communication skill level and the curriculum standard against which the student's progress is assessed?     PRAXIS 3          CEC 8
    A.  Special education teacher
    B.  Occupational therapist
    C.  Speech-language pathologist
    D.  Physical therapist

Now that you have completed your chapter study, go back to the chapter objectives and see if you have truly met them. You may want to write out your responses to the chapter objectives so that you can check your understanding against the chapter outline or the text.

# Chapter 7: Understanding Students with Emotional or Behavioral Disorders

## Objectives: Guiding Your Chapter Reading

The content in this chapter is presented to help you achieve the following objectives. Once you complete your study of the chapter, see if you can do what the objectives describe. If not, you may need to do some more reviewing of the chapter and your class notes.

- Define and identify the characteristics of students with emotional or behavioral disorders
- Recall the major causes of emotional or behavioral disorders
- Explain the assessment and evaluation practices for students with emotional or behavioral disorders
- Identify the major issues impacting students with emotional or behavioral disorders
- Describe successful instructional practices and accommodations for students with emotional or behavioral disorders

## Standards Matrices: Relating Content to Professional Standards

The matrices, or charts, below help you see how the professional standards from the Council for Exceptional Children (CEC) and PRAXIS™ apply to the content in this chapter. In addition, you can refer to the margin notes throughout the chapter and the activities at the end of each chapter to make sure you understand how these standards apply to the content in the field of special education. These standards are important for you to know because they provide the basis for the professional teacher certification examinations and content covered in these exams.

| CEC Standards | Chapter Topic |
|---|---|
| 1 | <ul><li>IDEA</li><li>Definition of emotional and behavioral disorders</li></ul> |
| 2 | <ul><li>Case study</li><li>Characteristics of emotional and behavioral disorders</li><li>Causes of emotional and behavioral disorders</li></ul> |
| 3 | <ul><li>Cognitive and academic characteristics</li><li>Supplementary aids and services</li><li>Universal design for learning</li><li>Testing accommodations</li><li>Inclusion</li></ul> |
| 4 | <ul><li>Universal design for learning</li><li>Effective strategies as they relate to early childhood, middle, and high school years</li></ul> |
| 5 | <ul><li>Planning for other educational needs</li><li>Conflict resolution</li><li>Inclusion</li></ul> |
| 6 | |
| 7 | <ul><li>Supplementary aids and services</li><li>Inclusion</li></ul> |
| 8 | <ul><li>Evaluation and assessment</li><li>Behavioral and Emotional Rating Scale</li><li>Measuring student progress</li></ul> |
| 9 | <ul><li>Characteristics of emotional and behavioral disorders</li><li>Partnering for special education and related services</li></ul> |
| 10 | <ul><li>Case study</li><li>Partnering for special education and related services</li><li>Wraparound collaboration</li><li>Planning for other educational needs</li><li>Inclusion</li></ul> |

| PRAXIS™ Standards | Chapter Topic |
|---|---|
| 1 | • Case study<br>• Characteristics of emotional and behavioral disorders<br>• Causes of emotional and behavioral disorders<br>• Cognitive and academic characteristics |
| 2 | • IDEA<br>• Definition of emotional and behavioral disorders |
| 3 | • Partnering for special education and related services<br>• Supplementary aids and services<br>• Universal design for learning<br>• Testing accommodations<br>• Evaluation and assessment<br>• Behavioral and Emotional Rating Scale<br>• Measuring student progress<br>• Wraparound collaboration<br>• Planning for other educational needs<br>• Inclusion |

## Checking for Understanding: Key Terms

To check that you understand the basic terms and vocabulary in the chapter, use the space provided to write the definitions or descriptions in your own words. Then, check the chapter to see how accurate your definition is, making sure you understand the context, or situation, in which the word is used. Reviewing these terms will help you better understand the concepts that support the content in this chapter.

| Term | Definition/Description | (✓) |
|---|---|---|
| anxiety disorder | | |
| separation anxiety disorder | | |
| generalized anxiety disorder | | |
| phobia | | |
| panic disorder | | |
| obsessive-compulsive disorder | | |

| | | |
|---|---|---|
| post-traumatic stress disorder | | |
| mood disorder | | |
| bipolar disorder | | |
| oppositional defiant disorder | | |
| conduct disorder | | |
| schizophrenia | | |
| externalizing behaviors | | |
| internalizing behaviors | | |
| child maltreatment | | |
| wraparound | | |
| reverse-role tutoring | | |
| classroom-centered intervention | | |
| service learning | | |

| Additional Term | | |
|---|---|---|
| conflict resolution | | |

## Chapter Outline: Taking Chapter Notes

The following outline is taken from the PowerPoint slides or overheads that your professor uses in class for this chapter. In the slides, there are several embedded links to more information for this chapter. Please go to the Companion Website at http://www.prenhall.com/turnbull to access them easily.

If you take your Student Study Guide to class, you can use this outline for taking notes on the chapter or for review. It will also allow you to listen to lectures and participate in class discussions without having to copy down all the PowerPoint information.

The notes below are set up for recording information from the chapter in a particular way—an adapted Cornell method of taking notes. In this adapted Cornell method, you underline, or highlight, information presented to you. In addition to highlighting, you can write information or explanations on the left-hand side of the table. Soon after the class presentation or reading the chapter, rewrite the notes from the left-hand side in your own words, using key terms and phrases. To study for quizzes or exams, you can cover up the left-hand side and use the right-hand side of the table to cue yourself about the information.

You also may just jot notes on the right-hand side to help you. Since this outline reduces the chapter for you, it will be a useful study aid. The summary at the end of the chapter is another useful resource to use for review.

| Chapter 7<br>Understanding Students with Emotional or<br>Behavioral Disorders | NOTES |
|---|---|
| [Slide 7-1] Chapter 7 Objectives: At the end of this chapter you should be able to:<br>• Define and identify the characteristics of students with emotional or behavioral disorders<br>• Recall the major causes of emotional or behavioral disorders<br>• Explain the assessment and evaluation practices for students with emotional or behavioral disorders<br>• Identify the major issues impacting students with emotional or behavioral disorders<br>• Describe successful instructional practices and accommodations for students with emotional or behavioral disorders | |

| | |
|---|---|
| [Slide 7-2] Who Is Matthew Ackinclose?<br>• A 14-year-old eighth-grade student<br>• Began having problems as early as infancy, demonstrating self-injurious behaviors<br>• Was taking up to 22 different medications<br>• At age 8, his mother made contact with a social worker who looked for his strengths, rather than focusing on his weaknesses.<br>• She found a teacher who was willing to work with Matthew as a student.<br>• She has also focused on his strengths and created an atmosphere of respect.<br>• She collaborates successfully with other teachers and professionals in order to allow Matthew to participate fully in typical age-appropriate activities. | |
| [Slide 7-3] Defining Emotional or Behavioral Disorders<br>• IDEA Definition of Emotional Disturbance<br>  ▪ Over a long time<br>  ▪ To a marked degree<br>  ▪ Adversely affects a child's educational performance<br>  ▪ Accompanied by one or more of 5 characteristics<br>  ▪ Includes schizophrenia, but does not apply to children who are socially maladjusted unless they also meet the other criteria for having an emotional disturbance | |
| [Slide 7-4] Prevalence of EBD<br>• Approximately 0.7 percent served<br>• Debate over accuracy of amount<br>• Gender, ethnic, and socioeconomic factors influence prevalence<br>  ▪ White males more than White females<br>  ▪ Black females more than White females<br>  ▪ Black males highest disproportionality<br>  ▪ More students with lower socioeconomic status | |

| | |
|---|---|
| [Slide 7-5] Emotional Characteristics of EBD (NIMH)<br>• Anxiety disorder<br>   ▪ Separation anxiety<br>   ▪ Generalized anxiety disorder<br>   ▪ Phobia<br>   ▪ Panic disorder<br>   ▪ Obsessive-compulsive disorder<br>   ▪ Post-traumatic stress disorder<br>• Mood disorder<br>   ▪ Depression,<br>   ▪ Suicide<br>   ▪ Bipolar<br>• Oppositional defiant disorder<br>• Conduct disorder<br>• Schizophrenia | |
| [Slide 7-6] Behavioral Characteristics of EBD<br>• Externalizing behaviors<br>   ▪ Aggression<br>   ▪ Acting out<br>   ▪ Noncompliant behaviors<br>• Internalizing behaviors<br>   ▪ Withdrawal<br>   ▪ Depression<br>   ▪ Anxiety<br>   ▪ Obsessions<br>   ▪ Compulsions<br>• Can occur simultaneously | |
| [Slide 7-7] Cognitive and Academic Characteristics of EBD<br>• Below grade level in reading, math, and writing<br>• Higher dropout rate<br>• Achievement more difficult with externalizing behaviors<br>• Less likely to attend postsecondary school<br>• Many have undiagnosed or diagnosed language deficits | |
| [Slide 7-8] Determining the Causes<br>• Biological Causes<br>• Environmental stressors<br>   ▪ May interact with biological causes<br>• Stressful living conditions<br>   ▪ Poverty<br>   ▪ Homelessness<br>• Child maltreatment<br>   ▪ Neglect<br>   ▪ Physical abuse<br>   ▪ Sexual abuse<br>   ▪ Emotional abuse<br>• School factors | |
| [Slide 7-9] Nondiscriminatory Evaluation Process (See Figure 7–2) | |

| | |
|---|---|
| [Slide 7-10] Determining the Presence<br>• Rating scales, personality inventories, and observations<br>    ▪ They did not always follow the IDEA definition<br>• Scale for Assessing Emotional Disturbance<br>    ▪ Follows 5 elements from IDEA<br>        • Inability to learn<br>        • Inability to build or maintain satisfactory relationships<br>        • Inappropriate behavior<br>        • Unhappiness or depression<br>        • Physical symptoms or fears<br>• Talk to student about his or her interests, preferences, and positive life experiences | |
| [Slide 7-11] Partnering for Special Education and Related Services<br>• Wraparound services:<br>    ▪ School, community, mental health, and other services are "wrapped around" the student instead of compartmentalized<br>        • Stabilize crisis<br>        • Orient family and student to wraparound process<br>        • Develop support planning team<br>        • Identify strengths, needs, culture, and vision<br>        • Create team mission and ground rules<br>        • Prioritize interventions, goals, and indicators<br>        • Identify strength-based strategies<br>        • Develop a crisis and safety plan<br>        • Track the plan's progress<br>    ▪ The Wraparound Fidelity Index assessment tool | |
| [Slide 7-12] Determining Supplementary Aids and Services<br>• Classwide, Peer-assisted Self-management<br>    ▪ Decreases disruptive behavior and maintains appropriate behaviors, even in the absence of a teacher<br>• Reverse role tutoring<br>    ▪ Using students with emotional or behavioral disorders as tutors for non-disabled peers | |

| | |
|---|---|
| [Slide 7-13] Planning for Universal Design for Learning<br>• Use a computer with word processing software<br>    ▪ Increases students' willingness to edit and correct their work<br>    ▪ Results in clean, legible products<br>• Talking word processors, alphabetical keyboards, or word prediction software may decrease frustration when writing | |
| [Slide 7-14] Planning for Other Educational Needs<br>• More than half drop out of high school<br>• Statistics two years later show low employment rate for dropouts<br>• Reasons for dropout rate<br>• Several interventions have been identified to reduce the dropout rate | |
| [Slide 7-15] Preventing Dropouts<br>• Establish a student advisory program<br>• Establish and involve students in extracurricular activities<br>• Systematically monitor risk factors associated with dropout<br>• Develop "schools within schools" or smaller units.<br>• Establish school-to-work programs<br>• Engage in community-based learning<br>• Use the "check and connect" strategy<br>• Provide vocational education | |
| [Slide 7-16] Early Childhood Students<br>• Classroom-centered intervention<br>• Family-school partnership intervention<br>• Combining both classroom-centered intervention and family-school partnership intervention may yield the greatest benefits | |
| [Slide 7-17] Elementary and Middle School Students<br>• Service Learning<br>    ▪ Includes active participation and structured reflection in organized activities to meet community needs<br>        • Positive consequences<br>        • Examples | |
| [Slide 7-18] Secondary and Transition Students<br>• In conflict resolution, students learn<br>    ▪ Effective communication<br>    ▪ Anger management<br>    ▪ Taking another's perspective<br>• Conflicts usually occur because of resources, needs, or goals<br>• Teaches problem solving and successful decision making | |

| | |
|---|---|
| [Slide 7-19] Educational Placement (See Figure 7–3) | |
| [Slide 7-20] Measuring Students' Progress<br>• Mastery learning (or mastery training)<br>    ▪ Frequently assess students' mastery of content, determining whether to move on to the next concept<br>    ▪ To monitor mastery, effective teachers will:<br>        • Ask questions of the whole class<br>        • Use a cooperative learning strategy such as "think-pair-share"<br>• Social Skills<br>    ▪ Use of social skills rating system<br>    ▪ Sociometric ratings for rankings | |
| [Slide 7-21] Making Accommodations for Assessment<br>• Students in alternative school settings need to progress in the general education curriculum so that they may return to their neighborhood schools<br>• Students with EBD may be more likely to have difficulty with testing due to heightened anxiety<br>• Appropriate testing accommodations include:<br>    ▪ Extended time for testing<br>    ▪ Individual test administration<br>    ▪ Breaks during testing | |
| [Slide 7-22] Looking to Matthew's Future<br>• Preparing to enter high school and work with new teachers<br>• Rebecca believes it will be "Matt's chance to shine"<br>• Still focusing on improving social skills and a more positive relationship with his family<br>• Planning to work with a work placement counselor during his junior year | |

## Activities: Applying Your Learning

Just as the textbook described Universal Design for Learning as the way for you to teach children, the principles work well for adult learners too. Rather than just taking notes, taking quizzes, and writing essays, the following activities will help you to learn the material on a deeper level and remember it better.

1. Externalizing and Internalizing Behaviors.  Most emotional and behavioral disorders are classified as possessing mostly externalizing or internalizing behaviors. Even though your textbook says that they may occur at the same time, list the disorders mentioned in the chapter that have externalizing behaviors and which have internalizing behaviors.

| Externalizing Behavior Disorders | Internalizing Behavior Disorders |
|---|---|
| | |

Which disorders have behaviors in both categories?

2. Suicide prevention. Here is an easy mnemonic to remember these warning signs from the American Association of Suicidology at suicidology.org:

**IS PATH WARM?**

| | |
|---|---|
| I | Ideation |
| S | Substance Abuse |
| P | Purposelessness |
| A | Anxiety |
| T | Trapped |
| H | Hopelessness |
| W | Withdrawal |
| A | Anger |
| R | Recklessness |
| M | Mood Changes |

What to Do: Here are some ways to be helpful to someone who is threatening suicide:

- Be direct. Talk openly and matter-of-factly about suicide.
- Be willing to listen. Allow expressions of feelings. Accept the feelings.
- Be non-judgmental. Don't debate whether suicide is right or wrong, or whether feelings are good or bad. Don't lecture on the value of life.
- Get involved. Become available. Show interest and support.
- Don't dare him or her to do it.
- Don't act shocked. This will put distance between you.
- Don't be sworn to secrecy. Seek support.
- Offer hope that alternatives are available but do not offer glib reassurance.
- Take action. Remove means, such as guns or stockpiled pills.
- Get help from persons or agencies specializing in crisis intervention and suicide prevention.

How can you make sure you remember how to respond to someone who is threatening suicide? On another piece of paper: a) write or draw a mnemonic; b) draw a picture; or c) write a poem, rap, or rhyme. Share it with the class. It may become an instructional tool worth sharing with colleagues and students.

3. Other interactive activities are available at the Companion Website found at http://www.prenhall.com/turnbull. There is a website for children to teach conflict management that is quite entertaining, called "Out on a Limb: A Guide to Getting Along." Two STAR Legacy modules give some in-depth instruction on "Addressing Disruption and Non-Compliant Behaviors" in the classroom. These modules are highly recommended for all teachers.

4. Do not forget the DVD cases packaged with your textbook. There you can see video clips of the individuals discussed in the book.

Use your *Real Lives & Exceptionalities* DVD to view *Project Success*, a service-learning program. Click on "Beyond School" to meet "Karen" (Clip 4), the *Project Success* director, as well as "Jamie" (Clip 5) and "Jonathan" (Clip 6), who participate in the program.

How successful do you believe service learning can be for students with emotional and behavioral disorders? Is this something that could be accomplished at most schools? Why or why not?

*The questions that correspond to the DVD case studies are on the DVD, but they are also found in the back of this Student Study Guide. This will allow you to see the questions ahead of time. You are also welcome to write notes or answer the questions before typing them on the DVD.*

## Practice Quiz: Assessing Your Knowledge

Below are some questions to help you review the content in the chapter. Answers to the questions are provided for you at the end of the Student Study Guide. Circle the correct answer for each question.

1. Which of the following is not an anxiety disorder?       PRAXIS 1       CEC 2
    A. Panic disorder
    B. Mood disorder
    C. Obsessive-compulsive disorder
    D. Post-traumatic stress disorder

2. Yasmine suffers frightening flashbacks of a bombing that occurred in her neighborhood. What kind of anxiety disorder best describes Yasmine?       PRAXIS 1       CEC 2
    A. Obsessive compulsive disorder
    B. Eating disorder
    C. Bipolar disorder
    D. Post-traumatic stress disorder

3. What term was defined as "the ability to emerge as a highly functioning adult despite growing up in extremely stressful circumstances"?       PRAXIS 1       CEC 5
    A. Resiliency
    B. Self-determination
    C. Self-actualization
    D. Conflict resolution

4. What disorder is characterized by exaggerated mood swings?       PRAXIS 1       CEC 2
    A. Panic disorder
    B. Eating disorder
    C. Bipolar disorder
    D. Conduct disorder

5. What approach is intended to provide information on student progress that teachers can use to modify instruction?  PRAXIS 3       CEC 3
    A. Mastery evaluation
    B. Direct instruction
    C. Mastery reading
    D. Teacher observation

6. What percentage of children who have language deficits also have emotional disorders?
          PRAXIS 1       CEC 2
    A. 40%
    B. 10%
    C. 49%
    D. Over 50%

7. Which of the following students may have an internalizing behavior concern?       PRAXIS 1       CEC 2
    A. Johann, who is noncompliant with adults
    B. Gustoff, who argues with adults and peers
    C. Stephan, who is withdrawn and appears sad
    D. Walter, who lies, steals, and has tantrums

8. When is a determining cause of an emotional/behavioral disorder useful, according to the authors?
          PRAXIS 1       CEC 3
    A. When the cause leads to a specific diagnostic label
    B. When the cause provides additional IDEA funding
    C. When the cause leads to interventions or preventions
    D. When the cause leads to a decrease in restrictive placements for these students

9. When observing Zerena, Ms. Green is interested only in knowing the length of Zerena's temper tantrum. Which observational system would be most useful?     PRAXIS 3          CEC 8
    A. Frequency
    B. Duration
    C. Latency
    D. Magnitude

10. Which method involves having students participate in structured activities that meet community needs?
             PRAXIS 3          CEC 4
    A. Conflict resolution
    B. Self-management
    C. Service learning
    D. Community involvement

11. What does DSM stand for?     PRAXIS 1          CEC 1
    A. Diagnostic Standardized Manual for Psychological Disorders
    B. Diagnostic and Statistical Manual of Mental Disorders
    C. Developmental Standards for Mental Disorders
    D. Deviant Standards for Mental Disorders

12. Which of the following is NOT a suggested practice when talking to a person who is suicidal?
             PRAXIS 3          CEC 2
    A. Take the person's comments seriously
    B. Point out that others have worse troubles
    C. Listen without judging
    D. Encourage the person to problem solve

13. Which of the following was listed as a reason for the underidentification of students with emotional or behavioral disorders? PRAXIS 1          CEC 3
    A. Subjectivity in the identification process
    B. Willingness to serve these students in the general education classroom
    C. Effective prereferral practices in the schools
    D. Wraparound counseling services in the schools

14. What are two rules of thumb for working with students with behavioral issues?     PRAXIS 3     CEC 3
    A. Begin early and use all the tools available
    B. Wait and see
    C. Use all available resources and medication
    D. Remove them from social situations with peers

15. One way teachers can assure that students with emotional issues are accepted by class members is to:
             PRAXIS 3          CEC 8
    A. Observe the students at play as they interact with one another
    B. Observe the students as they choose partners for various activities
    C. Ask students to identify classmates with whom they play and would like to play; tally the number of times any particular student is identified
    D. All of the above

Now that you have completed your chapter study, go back to the chapter objectives and see if you have truly met them. You may want to write out your responses to the chapter objectives so that you can check your understanding against the chapter outline or the text.

# Chapter 8: Understanding Students with Attention-Deficit/Hyperactivity Disorder

## Objectives: Guiding Your Chapter Reading

The content in this chapter is presented to help you achieve the following objectives. Once you complete your study of the chapter, see if you can do what the objectives describe. If not, you may need to do some more reviewing of the chapter and your class notes.

- Define and identify the characteristics of students with attention deficit/hyperactivity disorder
- Recall the major causes of attention deficit/hyperactivity disorder
- Explain the assessment and evaluation practices for students with attention deficit/hyperactivity disorder
- Identify the major issues impacting students with attention deficit/hyperactivity disorder
- Describe successful instructional practices and accommodations for students with attention deficit/hyperactivity disorder

## Standards Matrices: Relating Content to Professional Standards

The matrices, or charts, below help you see how the professional standards from the Council for Exceptional Children (CEC) and PRAXIS™ apply to the content in this chapter. In addition, you can refer to the margin notes throughout the chapter and the activities at the end of each chapter to make sure you understand how these standards apply to the content in the field of special education. These standards are important for you to know because they provide the basis for the professional teacher certification examinations and content covered in these exams.

| CEC Standards | Chapter Topic |
|---|---|
| 1 | <ul><li>IDEA</li><li>Definition of attention deficit/hyperactivity disorder</li></ul> |
| 2 | <ul><li>Case study</li><li>Characteristics of attention deficit/hyperactivity disorder</li><li>Behavioral, emotional, and social characteristics</li><li>Determining the causes of attention deficit/hyperactivity disorder</li></ul> |
| 3 | <ul><li>Intellectual functioning and academic achievement</li><li>Instruction and services</li><li>Universal design for learning</li><li>Testing accommodations</li><li>Inclusion</li></ul> |
| 4 | <ul><li>Universal design for learning</li><li>Effective strategies as they relate to early childhood, middle, and high school years</li></ul> |
| 5 | <ul><li>Instructional environment</li><li>Planning for other educational needs</li><li>Inclusion</li></ul> |
| 6 | |
| 7 | <ul><li>Supplementary aids and services</li><li>Inclusion</li></ul> |
| 8 | <ul><li>Evaluation and assessment of attention deficit/hyperactivity disorder</li><li>Measuring student progress</li></ul> |
| 9 | <ul><li>Characteristics of attention deficit/hyperactivity disorder</li><li>Partnering for special education and related services</li></ul> |
| 10 | <ul><li>Case study</li><li>Partnering for special education and related services</li><li>Planning for other educational needs</li><li>Inclusion</li></ul> |

| PRAXIS™ Standards | Chapter Topic |
|---|---|
| 1 | • Case study<br>• Characteristics of attention deficit/hyperactivity disorder<br>• Behavioral, social, and emotional characteristics<br>• Causes of attention deficit/hyperactivity disorder<br>• Intellectual functioning and academic achievement |
| 2 | • IDEA<br>• Definition of attention deficit/hyperactivity disorder |
| 3 | • Partnering for special education and related services<br>• Supplementary aids and services<br>• Universal design for learning<br>• Testing accommodations<br>• Evaluation and assessment<br>• Measuring student progress<br>• Planning for other educational needs<br>• Inclusion |

## Checking for Understanding: Key Terms

To check that you understand the basic terms and vocabulary in the chapter, use the space provided to write the definitions or descriptions in your own words. Then, check the chapter to see how accurate your definition is, making sure you understand the context, or situation, in which the word is used. Reviewing these terms will help you better understand the concepts that support the content in this chapter.

| Term | Definition/Description | (✓) |
|---|---|---|
| hyperactivity | | |
| impulsivity | | |
| nonverbal working memory | | |
| internalization of speech | | |
| self-regulation of affect, motivation, and arousal | | |
| reconstitution | | |

| | | |
|---|---|---|
| dopamine | | |
| neurotransmitters | | |
| neuroimaging | | |
| multimodal treatments | | |
| errorless learning | | |
| cognitive behavioral therapies | | |
| goal attainment scaling | | |
| T-chart | | |

## Chapter Outline: Taking Chapter Notes

The following outline is taken from the PowerPoint slides or overheads that your professor uses in class for this chapter. In the slides, there are several embedded links to more information for this chapter. Please go to the Companion Website at http://www.prenhall.com/turnbull to access them easily.

If you take your Student Study Guide to class, you can use this outline for taking notes on the chapter or for review. It will also allow you to listen to lectures and participate in class discussions without having to copy down all the PowerPoint information.

The notes below are set up for recording information from the chapter in a particular way—an adapted Cornell method of taking notes. In this adapted Cornell method, you underline, or highlight, information presented to you. In addition to highlighting, you can write information or explanations on the left-hand side of the table. Soon after the class presentation or reading the chapter, rewrite the notes from the left-hand side in your own words, using key terms and phrases. To study for quizzes or exams, you can cover up the left-hand side and use the right-hand side of the table to cue yourself about the information.

You also may just jot notes on the right-hand side to help you. Since this outline reduces the chapter for you, it will be a useful study aid. The summary at the end of the chapter is another useful resource to use for review.

| Chapter 8<br>Understanding Students with Attention-Deficit/Hyperactivity Disorder | NOTES |
|---|---|
| [Slide 8-1] Chapter 8 Objectives: At the end of this chapter you should be able to:<br>• Define and identify the characteristics of students with attention deficit/hyperactivity disorder<br>• Recall the major causes of attention deficit/hyperactivity disorder<br>• Explain the assessment and evaluation practices for students with attention deficit/hyperactivity disorder<br>• Identify the major issues impacting students with attention deficit/hyperactivity disorder<br>• Describe successful instructional practices and accommodations for students with attention deficit/hyperactivity disorder | |
| [Slide 8-2] Who is Kelsey Blankenship?<br>• Nine years old, living with her grandparents who adopted her<br>• Previously very active, surrounded by "commotion," problems with being patient and attentive<br>• Open to a treatment plan developed by a collaborative team made up of her teacher, therapist, psychiatrist, and grandparents<br>• Worked on developing better problem-solving skills<br>• Began taking prescribed medication<br>• Currently very involved in dramatic competitions and has much better interactions with her peers | |
| [Slide 8-3] Defining Attention-Deficit/Hyperactivity Disorder<br>• The condition must adversely impact the student's academic performance to receive services<br>• Students usually receive services under "other health impairments" since there is no IDEA category for ADHD<br>• APA definition<br>  ▪ Persistent pattern of inattention and/or hyperactivity-impulsivity more frequent and severe than typical<br>  ▪ Manifests before age 7, duration at least 6 months, present in 2 or more settings, not attributed to other disability | |

| | |
|---|---|
| [Slide 8-4] Prevalence of AD/HD<br>• Approximately 2 to 9% of school-age children have AD/HD<br>• Estimates vary widely because of differences in interpreting defining characteristics<br>• About three times as many boys than girls<br>• Latinos less likely to receive AD/HD diagnosis | |
| [Slide 8-5] Three subtypes of AD/HD<br>• Predominantly inattentive type<br>    ▪ Trouble paying attention, forgetful, easily distracted, selective attention<br>    ▪ Students may appear lethargic, apathetic, or hypoactive (move or respond too slowly)<br>    ▪ May be overlooked<br>• Predominantly hyperactive-impulsive type<br>    ▪ Cannot seem to sit still, talks excessively, difficulty playing quietly<br>    ▪ Few adolescents or adults have the HI type.<br>• Combined type<br>    ▪ Combines features of inattention and hyperactivity<br>    ▪ The majority of students with AD/HD are combined type | |
| [Slide 8-6] Deficits in Executive Functions<br>• Executive function includes being able to process information to make decisions, take actions, and solve problems.<br>• Four types of executive functions:<br>    ▪ Nonverbal working memory<br>    ▪ Internalization of speech<br>    ▪ Self-regulation of affect, motivation, and arousal<br>    ▪ Reconstitution | |
| [Slide 8-7] Intellectual Functioning and Academic Achievement<br>• Disagreement on the extent to which AD/HD affects intellectual functioning<br>• Due to executive functioning delays, students will have difficulty achieving academic success<br>• AD/HD characteristics can lead to positive aspects<br>    ▪ Hyperfocus | |

| | |
|---|---|
| [Slide 8-8] Behavioral, Social, and Emotional Characteristics<br>• May have a co-existing condition, including:<br>   ▪ Mood disorder, anxiety disorder, bipolar disorder, or obsessive-compulsive disorder<br>• Specific challenges may include:<br>   ▪ Conflicts with parents, teachers, and peers<br>   ▪ Low self-esteem<br>   ▪ Frequent rejection, low peer regard, difficulties making and keeping friends<br>   ▪ Higher rates of alcohol, tobacco, and substance dependence<br>   ▪ NOT an indicator of future delinquency | |
| [Slide 8-9] Determining the Causes<br>• Does NOT cause AD/HD<br>   ▪ Lack of self-control<br>   ▪ Poor parenting<br>   ▪ Too much television or video games<br>   ▪ Diet (sugar, aspartame, additives, preservatives, vitamins)<br>   ▪ Living in a fast-paced culture<br>• Heredity<br>   ▪ Focus on dopamine<br>• Brain differences<br>   ▪ Other biological causes | |
| [Slide 8-10] Nondiscriminatory Evaluation Process (See Figure 8–3) | |
| [Slide 8-11] Determining the Presence<br>• AD/HD determined by a pediatrician and a psychiatrist or psychologist<br>• Teachers may be asked to complete a behavior rating checklist as part of the evaluation<br>   ▪ CRS-R<br>• Once presence is already determined, there are assessments to help determine the nature and extent of services<br>   ▪ ADDES-3 | |

| | |
|---|---|
| [Slide 8-12] Partnering for Special Education and Related Services<br>• Not every student with AD/HD qualifies for IDEA services<br>    ▪ They may be able to receive services through Section 504<br>• One role of the IEP or 504 team is to develop educational plans that may or may not be in conjunction with medication<br>    ▪ Team members should never suggest a child needs medication. Only a doctor can make that determination.<br>    ▪ Teams also cannot make the taking of medication a requirement for attending school.<br>    ▪ Not all parents support the use of medication for their children. | |
| [Slide 8-13] Determining Supplementary Aids and Services<br>• Arrange the classroom in a consistent manner<br>• It is not always best to seat students with peers<br>• Seat the student in close proximity to the teacher<br>• Do not seat students with hyperactivity/impulsivity close to highly distracting areas<br>• Clearly post daily and weekly schedules<br>• Arrange the classroom to facilitate smooth transitions between classroom activities<br>• Clearly mark locations of storage for better organization<br>• Minimize classroom clutter | |
| [Slide 8-14] Designing an Appropriate IEP<br>• Planning for Universal Design for Learning<br>    ▪ Students need to learn organization and neatness<br>    ▪ Goal setting can improve organization skills<br>        • Identify and define a goal<br>        • Develop a series of objectives or tasks<br>        • Specify actions necessary to achieve desired outcomes<br>    ▪ Make goals challenging but obtainable<br>• Planning for Other Educational Needs<br>    ▪ Teachers should play a role in monitoring children on medication for changes or side effects | |

| | |
|---|---|
| [Slide 8-15] Early Childhood Students<br>• Multidisciplinary Diagnostic and Training Program<br>   ▪ Multimodal treatments<br>• Medication<br>• Parent Training<br>• Classroom Behavioral Management Interventions<br>   ▪ University of Florida MDTP<br>• Students initially attend diagnostic classrooms, then transition into general classrooms with ongoing support of AD/HD project teachers<br>• Project teachers collaborate with general educators and parents | |
| [Slide 8-16] Elementary and Middle School Students<br>• Errorless learning<br>   ▪ Presents discriminative stimuli and arranges the delivery of prompts in a learning situation in such a way as to ensure that the student gives only correct responses (or only a few incorrect responses)<br>   ▪ Prompts can be physical, verbal, or visual<br>   ▪ Premise is that learning that occurs without mistakes is stronger and lasts longer<br>• Use "most to least" prompting: most intrusive at first; then as task is mastered, prompts fade | |
| [Slide 8-17] Secondary and Transition Students<br>• Cognitive behavioral and self-control strategies<br>   ▪ Teach the use of inner speech, "self-talk"<br>   ▪ The purpose of cognitive behavioral strategies is to modify behavior and thinking patterns<br>   ▪ Possible benefits of this method are increased capacity for self-control and the self-regulation of behavior | |
| [Slide 8-18] Measuring Students' Progress<br>• Progress in the General Curriculum<br>   ▪ Curriculum-based management<br>   ▪ Goal Attainment Scaling (GAS) process<br>• Progress in Addressing Other Educational Needs<br>   ▪ Monitor progress in areas such as social skills, self-control, medication management<br>   ▪ T-charts<br>   ▪ Checklists | |

| | |
|---|---|
| [Slide 8-19] Making Accommodations for Assessment<br>• Issues include attention and concentration problems<br>    ▪ May qualify to take extra breaks<br>    ▪ May need multiple testing sessions<br>    ▪ May request a reduced-distraction testing environment | |
| [Slide 8-20] Looking to Kelsey's Future<br>• Kelsey would like to be a veterinarian.<br>• Her team supports her dream.<br>• She has begun making small steps toward that goal by succeeding in school, volunteering at the pound, and walking dogs.<br>• Her therapist envisions her developing skills to become a confident self-advocate. | |

## Activities: Applying Your Learning

Just as the textbook described Universal Design for Learning as the way for you to teach children, the principles work well for adult learners too. Rather than just taking notes, taking quizzes, and writing essays, the following activities will help you to learn the material on a deeper level and remember it better.

1. T-chart. The textbook describes a T-chart as an alternative assessment tool to checklists. In the T-chart provided below observe a person in your class, a person in a social situation, or a person in any public arena for 5 minutes. Write down what one type of the person's behaviors looks like and sounds like. This technique is used so teachers can record two aspects of one behavior at one time.

**Behavior:**

| Looks like | Sounds like |
|---|---|
| | |

Was this more difficult to complete than you thought? Would this be helpful data to have on a student with AD/HD? Why?

2. Goal setting. One of the suggestions offered in this chapter was to teach students goal setting. Choose one activity for a student to accomplish and describe how you will teach the steps of goal setting to the student?

| | |
|---|---|
| Identify and define a goal clearly and concretely. | |
| Develop a series of objectives or tasks to achieve the goal. | |
| Specify the actions necessary to achieve the desired outcome. | |

3. Other interactive activities are available at the Companion Website found at http://www.prenhall.com/turnbull. There is a simulation from "Misunderstood Minds" and videos of students with AD/HD discussing what life is like for them. Medication is discussed in some of the links. There are also several case studies to help you see what teachers can do to be successful with students with AD/HD.

4. Do not forget the DVD cases packaged with your textbook. There you can see video clips of the individuals discussed in the book.

Since many students have organizational problems, use your *Real Lives & Exceptionalities* DVD to review an organizational solution George's teacher implemented to help him find his materials faster. Click on, "Meet George," and then select "Accommodations" (Clip 2).

Would this idea work for students with organizational problems? What other ideas do you have for organization assistance?

*The questions that correspond to the DVD case studies are on the DVD, but they are also found in the back of this Student Study Guide. This will allow you to see the questions ahead of time. You are also welcome to write notes or answer the questions before typing them on the DVD.*

## Practice Quiz: Assessing Your Knowledge

Below are some questions to help you review the content in the chapter. Answers to the questions are provided for you at the end of the Student Study Guide. Circle the correct answer for each question.

1. Which educational environment is the most appropriate for most students with AD/HD?
   PRAXIS 1              CEC 2
   A. The resource room
   B. The general education classroom
   C. The learning lab
   D. The self-contained special education classroom

2. Which type of AD/HD is typically overlooked by teachers?      PRAXIS 1      CEC 2
   A. Inattentive type
   B. Hyperactive-impulsive type
   C. Combined type
   D. None of the above

3. Which child is primarily showing signs of hyperactivity?  PRAXIS 1              CEC 2
   A. Julia is forgetful in daily activities, does not follow through on tasks, and loses things frequently.
   B. Abe fidgets, is often on the go, and often leaves his seat and runs in the classroom.
   C. Sandy blurts out answers to questions, has difficulty waiting her turn, and interrupts others during games.
   D. Myrna does not seem to listen when spoken to, dislikes tasks that require sustained effort, and does not attend well to details.

4. What is the job of the nonverbal working memory?      PRAXIS 1              CEC 3
   A. To retrieve auditory, visual, and other past sensory images
   B. To remember social cues and behavioral expectations
   C. To retrieve ways to analyze and synthesize behaviors
   D. To provide the drive to be persistent in unmotivating tasks

5. Which executive function of the brain is associated with one's ability to persist in goal-directed activities in the presence of external rewards?  PRAXIS 3              CEC 2
   A. Nonverbal working memory
   B. Internalization of speech
   C. Self-regulation of affect, motivation, and arousal
   D. Reconstitution

6. Which term below refers to the child's ability to "lock onto a task—even to the point of being oblivious to other things in the environment"?      PRAXIS 1              CEC 2
   A. Concentration
   B. Attention
   C. Hyperfocus
   D. Metacognition

7. Which of the following was noted as a peri- or postnatal link to AD/HD?      PRAXIS 1      CEC 2
   A. Poor maternal nutrition during pregnancy
   B. Poor initial reading instruction
   C. Exposure to chemical poisons
   D. Recent parental divorce

8. Usually, who makes the initial diagnosis of AD/HD?      PRAXIS 1              CEC 2
   A. General education teacher, special education teacher, or parent
   B. Pediatrician, psychologist, or psychiatrist
   C. Psychologist, school counselor, or special education teacher
   D. Pediatrician, school counselor, school social worker

9. What percentage of students continues to face challenges related to AD/HD during their adult years?
   PRAXIS 1                CEC 2
   A. 20%
   B. 30%
   C. 50%
   D. 70%

10. Students with AD/HD may need test accommodations which may include:  PRAXIS 3        CEC 4
    A. Extra breaks
    B. Multiple sessions
    C. Distraction-free testing environments
    D. All of the above

11. For students with AD/HD, an inclusive placement may mean:        PRAXIS 3        CEC 4
    A. Stressful environment
    B. Difficulty making friends
    C. Pleasant learning environment
    D. Having friends

12. A frequently used evaluation tool to identify AD/HD is:  PRAXIS 1        CEC 8
    A. KTEA
    B. Conners' Rating Scales—Revised
    C. WISC III
    D. WIAT

13. What percentage of all children are identified as having AD/HD?  PRAXIS 1        CEC 2
    A. Between 10% and 20%
    B. Between 5% and 10%
    C. Over 12%
    D. Between 2% and 9%

14. Students learn that the way they think about themselves or a situation may be self-defeating. This is described as:  PRAXIS 3        CEC 3
    A. Cognitive distortions
    B. Cognitive awareness
    C. Self-service
    D. None of the above

15. Cognitive behavioral therapy is also referred to as:        PRAXIS 3        CEC 4
    A. Self-talk
    B. Self-modeling
    C. Self-awareness
    D. Knowledge of self

Now that you have completed your chapter study, go back to the chapter objectives and see if you have truly met them. You may want to write out your responses to the chapter objectives so that you can check your understanding against the chapter outline or the text.

# Chapter 9: Understanding Students with Mental Retardation

## Objectives: Guiding Your Chapter Reading

The content in this chapter is presented to help you achieve the following objectives. Once you complete your study of the chapter, see if you can do what the objectives describe. If not, you may need to do some more reviewing of the chapter and your class notes.

- Define and identify the characteristics of students with mental retardation
- Recall the major causes of mental retardation
- Explain the assessment and evaluation practices for students with mental retardation
- Identify the major issues impacting students with mental retardation
- Describe successful instructional practices and accommodations for students with mental retardation

## Standards Matrices: Relating Content to Professional Standards

The matrices, or charts, below help you see how the professional standards from the Council for Exceptional Children (CEC) and PRAXIS™ apply to the content in this chapter. In addition, you can refer to the margin notes throughout the chapter and the activities at the end of each chapter to make sure you understand how these standards apply to the content in the field of special education. These standards are important for you to know because they provide the basis for the professional teacher certification examinations and content covered in these exams.

| CEC Standards | Chapter Topic |
|---|---|
| 1 | <ul><li>IDEA</li><li>Definition of mental retardation</li></ul> |
| 2 | <ul><li>Case study</li><li>Characteristics of mental retardation</li><li>Determining the causes of mental retardation</li></ul> |
| 3 | <ul><li>Intellectual functioning and academic achievement</li><li>Instruction and services</li><li>Universal design</li><li>Testing accommodations</li><li>Inclusion</li><li>Community-based instruction</li></ul> |
| 4 | <ul><li>Universal design</li><li>Effective strategies as they relate to early childhood, middle school, and high school years</li><li>The Self-Determined Learning Model of Instruction</li><li>Community-based instruction</li></ul> |
| 5 | <ul><li>Instructional environment</li><li>Planning for other educational needs</li><li>Inclusion</li><li>Transition</li></ul> |
| 6 | <ul><li>Prelinguistic Milieu Teaching</li></ul> |
| 7 | <ul><li>Supplementary aids and services</li><li>Inclusion</li><li>Community-based instruction</li></ul> |
| 8 | <ul><li>Evaluation and assessment of mental retardation</li><li>Measuring student progress</li></ul> |
| 9 | <ul><li>Characteristics of mental retardation</li><li>Partnering for special education and related services</li></ul> |

| 10 | • Case study |
| | • Partnering for special education and related services |
| | • Planning for other educational needs |
| | • Inclusion |
| | • Community-based instruction |
| | • Transition |

| PRAXIS™ Standards | Chapter Topic |
|---|---|
| 1 | • Case study<br>• Characteristics of mental retardation<br>• Determining the causes of mental retardation<br>• Intellectual functioning and academic achievement |
| 2 | • IDEA<br>• Definition of mental retardation |
| 3 | • Partnering for special education and related services<br>• Supplementary aids and services<br>• Universal design<br>• Testing accommodations<br>• Evaluation and assessment<br>• Measuring student progress<br>• Planning for other educational needs<br>• Prelinguistic milieu teaching<br>• Inclusion<br>• Community-based instruction<br>• Transition |

## Checking for Understanding: Key Terms

To check that you understand the basic terms and vocabulary in the chapter, use the space provided to write the definitions or descriptions in your own words. Then, check the chapter to see how accurate your definition is, making sure you understand the context, or situation, in which the word is used. Reviewing these terms will help you better understand the concepts that support the content in this chapter.

| Term | Definition/Description | (✓) |
|---|---|---|
| short-term memory | | |
| generalization | | |
| outer-directedness | | |
| adaptive behavior | | |

| Term | Definition/Description | (✓) |
|---|---|---|
| self-determination | | |
| chromosomes | | |
| karyotyping | | |
| transition services | | |
| prelinguistic milieu teaching | | |
| life space analysis | | |
| ecological inventories | | |
| discrepancy analysis | | |
| activity task analysis | | |
| **Types of Support** | | |
| intermittent | | |
| limited | | |
| extensive | | |

| pervasive | | |
|---|---|---|
| | | |

## Chapter Outline: Taking Chapter Notes

The following outline is taken from the PowerPoint slides or overheads that your professor uses in class for this chapter. In the slides, there are several embedded links to more information for this chapter. Please go to the Companion Website at http://www.prenhall.com/turnbull to access them easily.

If you take your Student Study Guide to class, you can use this outline for taking notes on the chapter or for review. It will also allow you to listen to lectures and participate in class discussions without having to copy down all the PowerPoint information.

The notes below are set up for recording information from the chapter in a particular way—an adapted Cornell method of taking notes. In this adapted Cornell method, you underline, or highlight, information presented to you. In addition to highlighting, you can write information or explanations on the left-hand side of the table. Soon after the class presentation or reading the chapter, rewrite the notes from the left-hand side in your own words, using key terms and phrases. To study for quizzes or exams, you can cover up the left-hand side and use the right-hand side of the table to cue yourself about the information.

You also may just jot notes on the right-hand side to help you. Since this outline reduces the chapter for you, it will be a useful study aid. The summary at the end of the chapter is another useful resource to use for review.

| Chapter 9<br>Understanding Students with Mental Retardation | NOTES |
|---|---|
| [Slide 9-1] Chapter 9 Objectives: At the end of this chapter you should be able to:<br>• Define and identify the characteristics of students with mental retardation<br>• Recall the major causes of mental retardation<br>• Explain the assessment and evaluation practices for students with mental retardation<br>• Identify the major issues impacting students with mental retardation<br>• Describe successful instructional practices and accommodations for students with mental retardation | |

| | |
|---|---|
| [Slide 9-2] Who Is Erica Scott?<br>• Erica is 18 years old.<br>• She was born prematurely and also has cerebral palsy.<br>• She has been the center of collaboration efforts from her parents; two teachers, Teresa Pena and Kristen Zajicek; and other professionals<br>• Her father is currently serving in Iraq<br>• Erica will stay in school through age 21, and then work<br>• Her current curriculum focuses on functional skills she will need to live independently<br>• Students without disabilities have also learned how to interact with Erica | |
| [Slide 9-3] Defining Mental Retardation<br>• AAMR definition<br>  ▪ Mental retardation is a disability characterized by significant limitations both in intellectual functioning and in adaptive behavior as expressed in conceptual, social, and practical adaptive skills.<br>  ▪ This disability originates before age 18. | |
| [Slide 9-4] Five Assumptions Essential to the Application of the Definition (See Figure 9–1)<br>• Limitations in present functioning must be considered within the context of community environments typical of the individual's age peers and culture.<br>• Valid assessment considers cultural and linguistic diversity as well as differences in communication, sensory, motor, and behavioral factors.<br>• Within an individual, limitations often coexist with strengths.<br>• An important purpose of describing limitations is to develop a profile of needed supports.<br>• With appropriate personalized supports over a sustained period, the life functioning of the person with mental retardation generally will improve. | |
| [Slide 9-5] Definitions of Intensities of Support (See Figure 9–2)<br>• Intermittent: "As needed"<br>• Limited: Consistency, but time limited<br>• Extensive: Regular involvement (daily), not time limited<br>• Pervasive: Constancy, high intensity, potential life-sustaining nature | |

| | |
|---|---|
| [Slide 9-6] Prevalence of Mental Retardation<br>• Inconsistent rates, from 1% to 3% of the population<br>• U.S. Department of Education reported 0.9% in 2001<br>• In the 2003–2004 school year, 581,706 students with mental retardation, ages 6 to 21, received special education services | |
| [Slide 9-7] Characteristics of MR<br>• Limitations in Intellectual Functioning<br>  ▪ Measured through use of IQ tests<br>• Memory (short-term)<br>• Generalization<br>• Motivation (outer-directedness)<br>• Limitations in Adaptive Behavior<br>  ▪ Three domains: Conceptual Skills, Social Skills, Practical Skills<br>  ▪ Self-determination | |
| [Slide 9-8] Determining the Causes<br>• Causes by Timing<br>  ▪ Prenatal<br>  ▪ Perinatal<br>  ▪ Postnatal<br>• Causes by Type<br>  ▪ Biomedical<br>  ▪ Social<br>  ▪ Behavioral<br>  ▪ Educational | |
| [Slide 9-9] Nondiscriminatory Evaluation Process (See Figure 9–3) | |
| [Slide 9-10] Evaluating Students with Mental Retardation<br>• Determining the Presence<br>  ▪ Evaluate intellectual functioning and adaptive skills<br>    • Intellectual functioning: IQ tests<br>    • Adaptive skills: Measures such as AAMR Adaptive Behavior Scale—School<br>• Determining the Nature and Extent of General and Special Education and Related Services<br>  ▪ For older students, the Transition Planning Inventory is useful | |
| [Slide 9-11] AAMR 1983 Classifications (See Figure 9–4)<br>• These categories previously determined a child's classroom placement<br>• Categories now focus on needed levels of support | |

| | |
|---|---|
| [Slide 9-12] Partnering for Special Education and Related Services<br>• Transition Services<br>    ▪ Importance of transition services<br>    ▪ Student is the center of transition planning<br>    ▪ Parental input is important<br>    ▪ Include community agency representatives | |
| [Slide 9-13] Determining Supplementary Aids and Services<br>• Paraprofessionals<br>    ▪ Paraprofessionals can be important<br>    ▪ More than 280,000 in U.S.<br>    ▪ Paraprofessionals determine appropriate levels of support, issues about "protective bubble" effect, or "Velcro"<br>    ▪ Roles and Responsibilities | |
| [Slide 9-14] Planning for Universal Design for Learning<br>• Technology<br>    ▪ New programs help students improve their learning capacities<br>    ▪ CAST has developed programs that use UDL principles to teach reading<br>    ▪ Wiggle works in one reading program developed by CAST<br>    ▪ Another example of a free online reading program is at Starfall | |
| [Slide 9-15] Planning for Other Educational Needs<br>• Functional skills include:<br>    ▪ Applied money concepts<br>    ▪ Applied time concepts<br>    ▪ Community mobility and access<br>    ▪ Grooming and self-care<br>    ▪ Leisure activities<br>    ▪ Health and safety<br>    ▪ Career education<br>• Instruction in Inclusive Classrooms<br>• Instruction in Community Settings | |
| [Slide 9-16] Early Childhood Students<br>• Prelinguistic milieu teaching<br>• First, follow the child's lead<br>• Then, set the stage for communication<br>• Finally, be strategic when using games like Pat-a-Cake and Peek-a-Boo | |

| | |
|---|---|
| [Slide 9-17] Elementary and Middle School Students<br>• Self-determined learning model of instruction (the University of Kansas)<br>  ▪ 12 student questions<br>  ▪ Teacher objectives<br>  ▪ Educational supports<br>    • Three phases:<br>    • What is my goal?<br>    • What is my plan?<br>    • What have I learned? | |
| [Slide 9-18] Secondary and Transition Students—Community-Based Instruction<br>  ▪ Teaching in the natural environment<br>  ▪ Community-based Instructional Approaches<br>• "Learn it where you'll need to do it."<br>• "Teach it where you want your students to practice it."<br>  ▪ Project TASSEL has expanded to: TTAC | |
| [Slide 9-19] Educational Placement (See Figure 9–6) | |
| [Slide 9-20] Measuring Students' Progress<br>• Progress in the general curriculum<br>  ▪ Data-based monitoring: Requires teachers regularly to collect different types of data such as:<br>  ▪ Response-by-response data<br>  ▪ Instructional and test data<br>  ▪ Error data<br>  ▪ Anecdotal data | |
| [Slide 9-21] Measuring Students' Progress<br>• Progress in addressing other educational needs<br>  ▪ Ecological inventory process<br>• Life Space Analysis<br>  ▪ Gather information about the student's daily environments<br>  ▪ Conduct ecological inventories<br>  ▪ Conduct a discrepancy analysis<br>  ▪ Perform an activity task analysis | |
| [Slide 9-22] Making Accommodations for Assessment<br>• Accommodations may include:<br>  ▪ Dictating responses to someone<br>  ▪ Having extended time<br>  ▪ Having test items orally read<br>  ▪ Clarifying test items | |

| [Slide 9-23] Looking to Erica's Future | |
|---|---|
| • Erica's parents will continue to be strong allies for her<br>• She will leave school in three years and no longer have the support of her teachers<br>• She may begin a relationship with a vocational agency<br>• Perhaps she will attend a junior college<br>• She may capitalize upon her academic curriculum, her job-training, and her self-determination training | |

## Activities: Applying Your Learning

Just as the textbook described Universal Design for Learning as the way for you to teach children, the principles work well for adult learners too. Rather than just taking notes, taking quizzes, and writing essays, the following activities will help you to learn the material on a deeper level and remember it better.

1. Levels of support. Decorate the levels of support on the graphic organizer below. You can draw pictures, describe each in your own words, write key words, or provide examples of each.

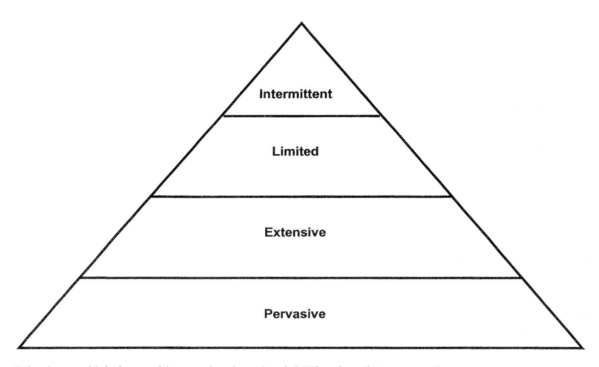

Why do you think the graphic organizer is a triangle? What does that represent?

Why is it important to view individuals with mental retardation by their level of need rather than their IQ level?

2. Self-determination. Let's try out the self-determination learning model of instruction. Fill out **Phase 1** and **Phase 2** of the form below for yourself in this class.

| Phase 1 Problem: What Is My Goal? | |
| --- | --- |
| 1. What do I want to learn? | |
| 2. What do I know about it? | |
| 3. What must change for me to learn what I don't know? | |
| 4. What can I do to make this happen? | |
| **Phase 2 Problem: What Is My Plan?** | |
| 5. What can I do to learn what I don't know? | |
| 6. What could keep me from taking action? | |

| 7. What can I do to remove these barriers? | |
|---|---|
| 8. When will I take action? | |

In a couple of weeks, come back and fill out Phase 3. Would this reflective process help individuals to take control of their own learning? Would it be helpful to individuals with mental retardation? Why?

| Phase 3 Problem: What Have I learned? | |
|---|---|
| 9. What actions have I taken? | |
| 10. What barriers have been removed? | |
| 11. What changed about what I did not know? | |
| 12. Do I know what I want to know? | |

3. Other interactive activities are available at the Companion Website found at http://www.prenhall.com/turnbull. There are several videos of individuals with mental retardation as well as case studies to illustrate how teachers can be successful with these students.

4. Do not forget the DVD cases packaged with your textbook. There you can see video clips of the individuals discussed in the book.

Use your *Real Lives & Exceptionalities* DVD to view Rachel, a career woman with Down syndrome. Click on "Beyond School" and then select "Rachel" (Clip 2). Why do you believe Rachel has been successful as a secretary?

*The questions that correspond to the DVD case studies are on the DVD, but they are also found in the back of this Student Study Guide. This will allow you to see the questions ahead of time. You are also welcome to write notes or answer the questions before typing them on the DVD.*

## Practice Quiz: Assessing Your Knowledge

Below are some questions to help you review the content in the chapter. Answers to the questions are provided for you at the end of the Student Study Guide. Circle the correct answer for each question.

1.  Which component in the IDEA definition of mental retardation refers to a measurable IQ of 70 or 75 or less?
    PRAXIS 2          CEC 1
    A.  Significantly subaverage general intellectual functioning
    B.  Deficits in adaptive behavior
    C.  Manifested during the developmental period
    D.  Below average academic skills

2.  Which of the following levels of support is the most intense?          PRAXIS 3          CEC 4
    A.  Limited
    B.  Pervasive
    C.  Extensive
    D.  Intermittent

3.  Which deficiency is being illustrated when Wesley is able to read the words *stop, yield,* and *crosswalk* in reading class, but he is unable to read these words on street signs as they appear in his neighborhood?
    PRAXIS 1          CEC 2
    A.  Below average intellectual skills
    B.  Below average adaptive skills
    C.  Poor generalization skills
    D.  Poor motivation skills

4.  Which of the following would be a consequence of a student who has very limited self-determination skills?
    PRAXIS 3          CEC 5
    A.  Positive self-concept
    B.  Outer-directedness
    C.  Limited verbal skills
    D.  Poor social skills

5.  Which of the following causes is usually associated with child abuse and child neglect?
    PRAXIS 1          CEC 2
    A.  Prenatal
    B.  Perinatal
    C.  Postnatal
    D.  All of the above

6.  A positive outcome for teaching self-determination skills to persons with mental retardation is:
    PRAXIS 3          CEC 5
    A.  High academic achievement
    B.  Regular high school diploma
    C.  Paid employment
    D.  None of the above

7.  Which one of the following areas is often assessed by interviewing individuals who are familiar with the person with mental retardation?          PRAXIS 3          CEC 8
    A.  Intelligence
    B.  Reading skills
    C.  Math skills
    D.  Adaptive behavior

8. Where should teacher Mr. Edwin teach the skill of comparison shopping if he wants his teaching to be as effective as possible? PRAXIS 3       CEC 5
    A. In the general education classroom
    B. In the special education classroom
    C. In the local grocery stores
    D. In the school's student lounge

9. What is the main purpose of a job coach? PRAXIS 3       CEC 5
    A. To assess the client's entry-level job skills
    B. To help the client complete required job forms
    C. To teach the client the skills for the job
    D. To assist the employer with any necessary job accommodations

10. For students with mental retardation, the IEP must include: PRAXIS 2       CEC 1
    A. IDEA
    B. Accommodations
    C. A and B
    D. Neither A nor B

11. Students with mental retardation receive higher academic gains in which type of classroom?
    PRAXIS 3       CEC 3
    A. Resource room
    B. General education classroom
    C. Self-contained classroom
    D. Separate facility

12. The philosophy that children will learn if their instruction matches their interests and abilities is known as:
    PRAXIS 3       CEC 4
    A. Prelinquistic milieu teaching
    B. Self-determination model
    C. Curriculum-based measurement
    D. Direct instruction

13. The adaptive behavior of students with mental retardation will: PRAXIS 1       CEC 2
    A. Fall below the norm
    B. Fall at the norm
    C. Fall above the norm
    D. None of the above

14. One characteristic of students with mental retardation is: PRAXIS 1       CEC 2
    A. Good receptive language
    B. Good expressive language
    C. Deficits in short-term memory
    D. None of the above

15. To have a label of mental retardation, the child must have an IQ of: PRAXIS 2       CEC 1
    A. 70 or below
    B. 85 or below
    C. 100 or below
    D. 130 or below

Now that you have completed your chapter study, go back to the chapter objectives and see if you have truly met them. You may want to write out your responses to the chapter objectives so that you can check your understanding against the chapter outline or the text.

# Chapter 10: Understanding Students with Severe and Multiple Disabilities

## Objectives: Guiding Your Chapter Reading

The content in this chapter is presented to help you achieve the following objectives. Once you complete your study of the chapter, see if you can do what the objectives describe. If not, you may need to do some more reviewing of the chapter and your class notes.

- Define and identify the characteristics of students with severe and multiple disabilities
- Recall the major causes of severe and multiple disabilities
- Explain the assessment and evaluation practices for students with severe and multiple disabilities
- Identify the major issues impacting students with severe and multiple disabilities
- Describe successful instructional practices and accommodations for students with severe and multiple disabilities

## Standards Matrices: Relating Content to Professional Standards

The matrices, or charts, below help you see how the professional standards from the Council for Exceptional Children (CEC) and PRAXIS™ apply to the content in this chapter. In addition, you can refer to the margin notes throughout the chapter and the activities at the end of each chapter to make sure you understand how these standards apply to the content in the field of special education. These standards are important for you to know because they provide the basis for the professional teacher certification examinations and content covered in these exams.

| CEC Standards | Chapter Topic |
|---|---|
| 1 | <ul><li>IDEA</li><li>Definition</li></ul> |
| 2 | <ul><li>Case study</li><li>Characteristics of severe and multiple disabilities</li><li>Causes of severe and multiple disabilities</li></ul> |
| 3 | <ul><li>Intellectual functioning</li><li>Supplementary aids and services</li><li>Universal design</li><li>Testing accommodations</li><li>Circle of Inclusion</li><li>MAPs</li></ul> |
| 4 | <ul><li>Universal design</li><li>Effective strategies as they relate to early childhood, middle school, and high school years</li></ul> |
| 5 | <ul><li>Planning for other educational needs</li><li>Inclusion</li><li>Circle of Inclusion</li></ul> |
| 6 | <ul><li>Assistive technology</li></ul> |
| 7 | <ul><li>Supplementary aids and services</li><li>Inclusion</li><li>Circle of Inclusion</li></ul> |
| 8 | <ul><li>Evaluation and assessment</li><li>Measuring student progress</li><li>Portfolio</li></ul> |
| 9 | <ul><li>Characteristics of severe and multiple disabilities</li><li>Partnering for special education and related services</li><li>MAPs</li></ul> |

| 10 | • Case study |
| | • Partnering for special education and related services |
| | • Planning for other educational needs |
| | • Inclusion |
| | • Circle of Inclusion |
| | • MAPs |

| PRAXIS™ Standards | Chapter Topic |
|---|---|
| 1 | • Case study<br>• Characteristics of severe and multiple disabilities<br>• Causes of severe and multiple disabilities<br>• Cognitive and academic characteristics |
| 2 | • IDEA<br>• Definition of severe and multiple disabilities |
| 3 | • Partnering for special education and related services<br>• Supplementary aids and services<br>• Universal design<br>• Testing accommodations<br>• Evaluation and assessment<br>• Portfolio<br>• Measuring student progress<br>• Planning for other educational needs<br>• Inclusion<br>• Circle of Inclusion<br>• MAPs |

## Checking for Understanding: Key Terms

To check that you understand the basic terms and vocabulary in the chapter, use the space provided to write the definitions or descriptions in your own words. Then, check the chapter to see how accurate your definition is, making sure you understand the context, or situation, in which the word is used. Reviewing these terms will help you better understand the concepts that support the content in this chapter.

| Term | Definition/Description | (✓) |
|---|---|---|
| Apgar test | | |
| MAPs | | |
| Peer tutoring | | |
| augmentative and alternative communication (AAC) | | |

| Term | Definition/Description | (✓) |
|---|---|---|
| partial participation | | |
| student-directed learning strategies | | |
| picture prompts or antecedent regulation strategies | | |
| self-instruction strategies | | |
| self-monitoring strategies | | |
| formative analysis | | |
| summative evaluation | | |
| field observation | | |
| time sampling | | |
| event recording | | |
| absence seizures | | |

## Chapter Outline: Taking Chapter Notes

The following outline is taken from the PowerPoint slides or overheads that your professor uses in class for this chapter. In the slides, there are several embedded links to more information for this chapter. Please go to the Companion Website at http://www.prenhall.com/turnbull to access them easily.

If you take your Student Study Guide to class, you can use this outline for taking notes on the chapter or for review. It will also allow you to listen to lectures and participate in class discussions without having to copy down all the PowerPoint information.

The notes below are set up for recording information from the chapter in a particular way—an adapted Cornell method of taking notes. In this adapted Cornell method, you underline, or highlight, information presented to you. In addition to highlighting, you can write information or explanations on the left-hand side of the table. Soon after the class presentation or reading the chapter, rewrite the notes from the left-hand side in your own words, using key terms and phrases. To study for quizzes or exams, you can cover up the left-hand side and use the right-hand side of the table to cue yourself about the information.

You also may just jot notes on the right-hand side to help you. Since this outline reduces the chapter for you, it will be a useful study aid. The summary at the end of the chapter is another useful resource to use for review.

| Chapter 10<br>Understanding Students with Severe and Multiple Disabilities | NOTES |
|---|---|
| [Slide 10-1] Chapter 10 Objectives: At the end of this chapter you should be able to:<br>• Define and identify the characteristics of students with severe and multiple disabilities<br>• Recall the major causes of severe and multiple disabilities<br>• Explain the assessment and evaluation practices for students with severe and multiple disabilities<br>• Identify the major issues impacting students with severe and multiple disabilities<br>• Describe successful instructional practices and accommodations for students with severe and multiple disabilities | |
| [Slide 10-2] Who Is Sierra Smith?<br>• Sierra is a 6-year-old girl<br>• She is the only child in all of New Mexico, and one of only about 500 in the entire world, who have a recorded (documented) Smith-Megenis syndrome (SMS)<br>• Sierra's parents say that she is a bookworm, always absorbing from the printed page or her computer-assisted toys<br>• In school, she is in an inclusion program<br>• She has severe behavioral problems and self-injurious behaviors<br>• She mouths objects and is not yet toilet-trained<br>• Her sleep cycle is inverted, and she has less stamina than other children<br>• Her relationship with her educators is co-dependent and she needs to develop more independence<br>• Her teachers are focusing on collaboration in order to strengthen her independence | |

| | |
|---|---|
| [Slide 10-3] Defining Severe and Multiple Disabilities<br>• No single definition covers all conditions<br>• IDEA defines multiple disabilities and severe disabilities in two definitions<br>• Two characteristics common to the different definitions:<br>  ▪ Extent of support required<br>• Usually extensive or pervasive<br>  ▪ Two or more disabilities typically occur simultaneously | |
| [Slide 10-4] Characteristics<br>• Intellectual functioning<br>  ▪ Most have significant intellectual impairments<br>• Adaptive skills<br>  ▪ Development of self-care skills is crucial<br>• Motor development<br>  ▪ Teachers need to be aware of student positioning<br>• Sensory functioning<br>  ▪ Many students have sensory impairments<br>• Communication skills<br>  ▪ Students with impaired communication skills may demonstrate needs and wants through inappropriate behaviors | |
| [Slide 10-5] Determining the Causes<br>• Biological causes account for about three-quarters of cases<br>• Severe mental retardation caused by:<br>  ▪ Genetic factors (22%)<br>  ▪ Chromosomal disorders (21%)<br>  ▪ Developmental brain abnormalities (9%)<br>  ▪ Inborn errors of metabolism and neuro-degenerative disorders (8%)<br>• Complications during and after birth also account for many severe disabilities<br>• Human Genome Project<br>• Apgar test—first test given to newborns | |
| [Slide 10-6] Nondiscriminatory Evaluation Process (See Figure 10–1) | |

| | |
|---|---|
| [Slide 10-7] Assistive Technology<br>The student's evaluation team should ensure that assistive technology devices:<br><ul><li>Are necessary for the student to make progress in the general curriculum.</li><li>Meet the IDEA definition, which defines AT as any item that is used with the student to increase, maintain, or improve functional capabilities.</li><li>Are considered appropriate for the environments in which the student participates.</li><li>Are examined through procedures that lead to potentially effective interventions.</li></ul> | |
| [Slide 10-8] Assistive Technology<br><ul><li>Assistive technology evaluations typically are multidisciplinary</li></ul>The team should consider:<br><ul><li>A speech, language, and communication assessment</li><li>A seating and positioning assessment</li><li>A mobility assessment</li><li>A switch use and input/output device assessment</li><li>A writing evaluation, hand and grip strength, fine motor skills</li><li>A visual and hearing assessment</li><li>An assessment of home, school, and community environment</li></ul><ul><li>SETT Framework</li></ul> | |
| [Slide 10-9] Partnering for Special Education and Related Services<br><ul><li>Making Action Plans (MAPs)<ul><li>What is MAPs?</li><li>What is your history or story?</li><li>What are your dreams?</li><li>What are your nightmares?</li><li>Who are you?</li><li>What are your strengths, gifts, and talents?</li><li>What do you need?</li><li>What is the plan of action?</li></ul></li></ul> | |

| | |
|---|---|
| [Slide 10-10] Determining Supplementary Aids and Services<br>• Peer tutoring—involves pairing students one-on-one<br>    ▪ Considerations in peer tutoring:<br>        • Relying too much on students without disabilities<br>        • Help is not and should never be the only basis for friendship<br>        • Unless help is reciprocal, the inherent inequity between tutor and tutee can distort the authenticity of a relationship | |
| [Slide 10-11] Planning for Universal Design for Learning<br>• Palmtop technologies<br>    ▪ Visual Assistant® Handheld Portable Prompter<br>    ▪ Hand-held Computers<br>    ▪ Allow students to complete multi-step tasks<br>    ▪ Prompts can be audio, visual, graphical<br>    ▪ Can be repeated as often as necessary | |
| [Slide 10-12] Planning for Other Educational Needs<br>• Augmentative and Alternative Communication (AAC)<br>    ▪ The devices, techniques, and strategies used by students who are unable to communicate fully through natural speech and/or writing<br>    ▪ May also include a wide array of options for communication, from low-tech message boards, symbols, pictures, and visual prompts to very complex technology (Examples)<br>    ▪ AAC devices have four key features:<br>        • Symbols<br>        • Displays<br>        • Selection options<br>        • Output modes | |

| | |
|---|---|
| [Slide 10-13] Early Childhood Students<br>• Circle of Inclusion, the University of Kansas<br>• A value-based commitment to including students with significant disabilities in programs available to typically developing children<br>• Friendships between young children with and without disabilities<br>• Collaboration among all parents and professionals<br>• Development of children's choice-making skills<br>• Use of the MAPs process<br>• Ongoing evaluation of how to make inclusion work<br>• Child-initiated, child-centered, developmentally-appropriate education | |
| [Slide 10-14] Elementary and Middle School Students<br>• Partial Participation Principle<br>  ▪ What noninstructional supports does the student need for meaningful participation?<br>  ▪ How much does the student wish to participate?<br>  ▪ How can teachers enhance the student's independence?<br>  ▪ Task Analysis | |
| [Slide 10-15] Secondary and Transition Students<br>• Student-Directed Learning Strategies<br>  ▪ Teach students with and without disabilities to modify and regulate their own learning<br>  ▪ Three important educational supports for students with severe disabilities:<br>    • Picture prompts or antecedent cue regulation<br>    • Self-instruction strategies<br>    • Self-monitoring strategies | |
| [Slide 10-16] Educational Placement (See Figure 10–5) | |
| [Slide 10-17] Strategies for Inclusion<br>• Collaborating among teachers and parents at all levels<br>• Teaching new skills in general education classrooms<br>• Promoting friendships in inclusive settings<br>• Facilitating positive outcomes for non-disabled peers<br>• Adapting the student's curriculum | |

| | |
|---|---|
| [Slide 10-18] Measuring Students' Progress<br>• General Curriculum<br>    ▪ Data-based decision-making<br>    ▪ Portfolio-based assessment<br>• Other Educational Needs<br>    ▪ Live observational methods include field observations, time sampling, and event recording<br>    ▪ Data collected includes frequency counts, duration data, and latency data | |
| [Slide 10-19] Making Accommodations for Assessment<br>• Alternate assessments<br>    ▪ Serve the same purpose as the typical accountability assessment<br>• Other formats for alternative assessments such as:<br>    ▪ IEP-linked body of evidence<br>    ▪ Performance assessment<br>    ▪ Checklist<br>    ▪ Portfolio-based alternate assessment<br>• Alternate assessment also relies on scoring criteria | |
| [Slide 10-20] Looking to Sierra's Future<br>• Sierra is "unfinished"<br>• She is currently developing across many areas, but mainly behavior<br>• Self-care and additional communication skills are also important<br>• Her education team sees inclusion as important because of the good peer models<br>• Her parents hope to see her more independent | |

## Activities: Applying Your Learning

Just as the textbook described Universal Design for Learning as the way for you to teach children, the principles work well for adult learners too. Rather than just taking notes, taking quizzes, and writing essays, the following activities will help you to learn the material on a deeper level and remember it better.

1. Making Action Plans. What are your goals in life and how do you plan on achieving them? This activity will take some time but is definitely worth doing. On another piece of paper, get together with another person you know and go through the MAPs process. This is even better if you can do it with a small group of your family or friends. Each person answers the questions about you! There is a recorder who writes down the answers but usually in a graphic organizer (a mind map) or by drawing pictures. At the end you come up with a "MAP" of your life, including your past, your present, and your future. It is a powerful experience for anyone and can be extremely useful for individuals with disabilities.

Making Action Plans (MAPs)
What is MAPs?
What is your history or story?
What are your dreams?
What are your nightmares?
Who are you?
What are your strengths, gifts, and talents?
What do you need?
What is the plan of action?

2. Partial participation. What does partial participation mean? Does it mean that a person with severe or multiple disabilities is just a spectator to life? Describe three activities and how they could be adjusted to allow the maximum amount of participation for an individual with severe or multiple disabilities.

| School activity: | Partial Participation: |
|---|---|
| Recreational activity: | Partial Participation: |
| Personal care activity: | Partial Participation: |

3. Other interactive activities are available at the Companion Website found at http://www.prenhall.com/turnbull. There are several videos of individuals with severe and multiple disabilities as well as case studies to illustrate how teachers can be successful with these students. There is also additional information about assistive technology and AAC devices.

4. Do not forget the DVD cases packaged with your textbook. There you can see video clips of the individuals discussed in the book.

Use your *Real Lives & Exceptionalities* DVD to revisit Star, who has multiple disabilities. How has she enriched the lives of the educators and service professionals she has encountered?

*The questions that correspond to the DVD case studies are on the DVD, but they are also found in the back of this Student Study Guide. This will allow you to see the questions ahead of time. You are also welcome to write notes or answer the questions before typing them on the DVD.*

## Practice Quiz: Assessing Your Knowledge

Below are some questions to help you review the content in the chapter. Answers to the questions are provided for you at the end of the Student Study Guide. Circle the correct answer for each question.

1. According to the IDEA definition of severe disabilities, which types of services might these children require?
   PRAXIS 2          CEC 1
   A. Specialized education services
   B. Psychological services
   C. Medical services
   D. All of the above

2. Which two concomitant impairments were not included in the IDEA definition of severe disabilities?
   PRAXIS 2          CEC 1
   A. Deaf-blindness
   B. Mental retardation–blindness
   C. Learning disability–attention deficit disorder
   D. Cerebral palsy–deafness

3. Which characteristic category associated with severe and multiple disabilities refers to areas such as dressing, personal grooming, feeding, and toileting?     PRAXIS 1          CEC 2
   A. Intellectual functioning
   B. Adaptive skills
   C. Motor development
   D. Sensory impairments

4. Which characteristic category associated with severe and multiple disabilities refers to challenges associated with muscle tone and spasticity?     PRAXIS 1          CEC 2
   A. Intellectual functioning
   B. Adaptive skills
   C. Motor development
   D. Sensory impairments

5. What international effort completed its attempt to identify all the human genes by the year 2003?
   PRAXIS 3          CEC 2
   A. The Human Genome Project
   B. The Gene Mapping Project
   C. The Health and Genetics Project
   D. The Genetic Disorders Research Project

6. Which cumulative score on the Apgar test signals that the baby may be at risk for developing disabilities?
   PRAXIS 1          CEC 2
   A. 4
   B. 7
   C. 25
   D. 70

7. Which question in the MAPs process allows participants to share their "great expectations" for the child?
   PRAXIS 3          CEC 5
   A. Who are you?
   B. What is your history or story?
   C. What are your dreams?
   D. What are your strengths, gifts, and talents?

8. In which setting do parents of children with severe and multiple disabilities believe their child will have a better chance of learning academic and functional skills?  PRAXIS 3      CEC 3
    A. The general education classroom
    B. The special education classroom
    C. The home setting
    D. The community

9. Why is the prereferral step often not used with individuals with severe or multiple disabilities?
        PRAXIS 3        CEC 8
    A. Because prereferral is not required by law
    B. Because the severity of the disability indicates a need for special education
    C. Because a medical diagnosis negates the reason for having prereferral
    D. Because these students do not begin their education in a general education setting

10. How did secondary general educators feel about their preparation to teach students with severe or multiple disabilities?  PRAXIS 3        CEC 9
    A. They felt very well prepared.
    B. They felt well prepared.
    C. They felt adequately prepared.
    D. They felt poorly prepared.

11. Which of the following was NOT a feature of the Circle of Inclusion program?      PRAXIS 3      CEC 5
    A. Ongoing evaluation to determine if inclusion is working
    B. Placing students in inclusive environments once they reach certain developmental milestones
    C. Developing children's choice-making skills
    D. Providing a child-initiated education

12. Compilation of a student's work for assessment purposes is called: PRAXIS 3        CEC 8
    A. Portfolio
    B. Assessment
    C. Alternative assessment
    D. Progress report

13. What percentage of students with severe and multiple disabilities are served in separate classrooms?
        PRAXIS 1        CEC 3
    A. About 25%
    B. About 30%
    C. About 50%
    D. Less than 15%

14. What screening test is used at birth?      PRAXIS 1        CEC 2
    A. Apgar
    B. Baley Scales
    C. WISC
    D. Vineland

15. Students with severe or multiple disabilities require:      PRAXIS 3        CEC 3
    A. Extensive supports
    B. Pervasive supports
    C. Indirect instructional supports
    D. A and B

Now that you have completed your chapter study, go back to the chapter objectives and see if you have truly met them. You may want to write out your responses to the chapter objectives so that you can check your understanding against the chapter outline or the text.

# Chapter 11: Understanding Students with Autism

## Objectives: Guiding Your Chapter Reading

The content in this chapter is presented to help you achieve the following objectives. Once you complete your study of the chapter, see if you can do what the objectives describe. If not, you may need to do some more reviewing of the chapter and your class notes.

- Define and identify the characteristics of students with autism
- Recall the major causes of autism
- Explain the assessment and evaluation practices for students with autism
- Identify the major issues impacting students with autism
- Describe successful instructional practices and accommodations for students with autism

## Standards Matrices: Relating Content to Professional Standards

The matrices, or charts, below help you see how the professional standards from the Council for Exceptional Children (CEC) and PRAXIS™ apply to the content in this chapter. In addition, you can refer to the margin notes throughout the chapter and the activities at the end of each chapter to make sure you understand how these standards apply to the content in the field of special education. These standards are important for you to know because they provide the basis for the professional teacher certification examinations and content covered in these exams.

| CEC Standards | Chapter Topic |
|---|---|
| 1 | <ul><li>IDEA</li><li>Definition</li></ul> |
| 2 | <ul><li>Case study</li><li>Characteristics of autism</li><li>Causes of autism</li></ul> |
| 3 | <ul><li>Differences in intellectual functioning</li><li>Supplementary aids and services</li><li>Universal design</li><li>Testing accommodations</li></ul> |
| 4 | <ul><li>Universal design</li><li>Effective strategies as they relate to early childhood, middle, and high school years</li><li>Mnemonic strategies</li><li>Social stories</li></ul> |
| 5 | <ul><li>Planning for other educational needs</li><li>Promoting friendships</li><li>Inclusion</li><li>Social stories</li><li>Positive behavior support</li></ul> |
| 6 | <ul><li>Delayed language functioning</li><li>Echolalia</li></ul> |
| 7 | <ul><li>Supplementary aids and services</li><li>Inclusion</li><li>Circle of Inclusion</li></ul> |
| 8 | <ul><li>Evaluation and assessment</li><li>Functional behavioral assessment</li><li>Measuring student progress</li><li>Discrete trial training</li></ul> |

| 9 | • Characteristics of autism |
| | • Functional behavior assessment |
| | • Positive behavior support |
| | • Social stories |
| | • Discrete trial training |
| | • Partnering for special education and related services |
| 10 | • Case study |
| | • Partnering for special education and related services |
| | • Planning for other educational needs |
| | • Inclusion |

| PRAXIS™ Standards | Chapter Topic |
|---|---|
| 1 | • Case study |
| | • Characteristics of autism |
| | • Causes of autism |
| | • Differences in intellectual functioning |
| 2 | • IDEA |
| | • Definition of autism |
| 3 | • Partnering for special education and related services |
| | • Supplementary aids and services |
| | • Universal design |
| | • Testing accommodations |
| | • Evaluation and assessment |
| | • Functional behavior assessment |
| | • Positive behavior support |
| | • Measuring student progress |
| | • Planning for other educational needs |
| | • Inclusion |
| | • Mnemonics |
| | • Social stories |
| | • Discrete trial training |

## Checking for Understanding: Key Terms

To check that you understand the basic terms and vocabulary in the chapter, use the space provided to write the definitions or descriptions in your own words. Then, check the chapter to see how accurate your definition is, making sure you understand the context, or situation, in which the word is used. Reviewing these terms will help you better understand the concepts that support the content in this chapter.

| Term | Definition/Description | (✓) |
|---|---|---|
| pervasive developmental disorders | | |
| autism spectrum disorder | | |

| | | |
|---|---|---|
| Asperger syndrome | | |
| echolalia | | |
| repetitive behavior | | |
| obsessions | | |
| tics | | |
| perseveration | | |
| savant syndrome | | |
| functional behavioral assessment | | |
| keyword strategies | | |
| pegword strategies | | |
| letter strategies | | |
| social stories | | |
| positive behavioral support | | |

| | | |
|---|---|---|
| applied behavioral analysis | | |
| discrete trial training | | |

## Chapter Outline: Taking Chapter Notes

The following outline is taken from the PowerPoint slides or overheads that your professor uses in class for this chapter. In the slides, there are several embedded links to more information for this chapter. Please go to the Companion Website at http://www.prenhall.com/turnbull to access them easily.

If you take your Student Study Guide to class, you can use this outline for taking notes on the chapter or for review. It will also allow you to listen to lectures and participate in class discussions without having to copy down all the PowerPoint information.

The notes below are set up for recording information from the chapter in a particular way—an adapted Cornell method of taking notes. In this adapted Cornell method, you underline, or highlight, information presented to you. In addition to highlighting, you can write information or explanations on the left-hand side of the table. Soon after the class presentation or reading the chapter, rewrite the notes from the left-hand side in your own words, using key terms and phrases. To study for quizzes or exams, you can cover up the left-hand side and use the right-hand side of the table to cue yourself about the information.

You also may just jot notes on the right-hand side to help you. Since this outline reduces the chapter for you, it will be a useful study aid. The summary at the end of the chapter is another useful resource to use for review.

| Chapter 11<br>Understanding Students with Autism | NOTES |
|---|---|
| [Slide 11-1] Chapter 11 Objectives: At the end of this chapter you should be able to:<br>• Define and identify the characteristics of students with autism<br>• Recall the major causes of autism<br>• Explain the assessment and evaluation practices for students with autism<br>• Identify the major issues impacting students with autism<br>• Describe successful instructional practices and accommodations for students with autism | |
| [Slide 11-2] Who Is Jeremy Jones?<br>• Jeremy is a 13-year-old boy with excellent mapping skills.<br>• He rehearses his necessary social skills without prompting.<br>• Using schoolwide positive behavior supports, Jeremy has been included in the general curriculum.<br>• He exhibits some common characteristics typical of students with autism. | |

| | |
|---|---|
| [Slide 11-3] Defining Autism<br>• IDEA: Autism is a developmental disability that affects children prior to the age of three in three areas:<br>    ▪ Verbal and nonverbal communication<br>    ▪ Social interaction<br>    ▪ Academic performance<br>• Diagnostic and Statistical Manual of Mental Disorders: Pervasive Developmental Disorder (PDD)<br>• Autism is a spectrum disorder, including Asperger syndrome | |
| [Slide 11-4] Prevalence of Autism<br>• In 2003–2004, 132,333 students<br>• Fewer students with Asperger syndrome<br>• Males outnumber females four to one<br>• Increased prevalence in last decade<br>• Different theories for the increase in prevalence:<br>    ▪ Greater public awareness<br>    ▪ More refined diagnostic procedures<br>    ▪ The alleged negative effect of vaccines (especially containing mercury) on young children's brain development | |
| [Slide 11-5] Characteristics of Autism<br>• Language Development<br>    ▪ Ranging from no verbal communication to complex communication<br>        • Delayed Language<br>        • Echolalia<br>• Social Development<br>    ▪ Delays in social interaction and social skills<br>        • Impaired use of nonverbal behavior<br>        • Lack of peer relationships<br>        • Failure to spontaneously share enjoyment, interests, and achievements<br>        • Lack of reciprocity | |
| [Slide 11-6] Characteristics of Autism<br>• Repetitive behavior<br>    ▪ Obsessions, tics, and perseverations<br>• Problem behavior<br>    ▪ Self-injurious behavior<br>    ▪ Aggression<br>• Need for environmental predictability<br>• Sensory and movement disorders<br>• Intellectual functioning<br>• Savant syndrome | |

| | |
|---|---|
| [Slide 11-7] Determining the Causes<br>• Historical perspectives on causes<br> ▪ "Refrigerator mothers"<br>• Biomedical causes<br> ▪ Abnormalities in brain development<br> ▪ Neurochemistry<br> ▪ Genetic factors | |
| [Slide 11-8] Nondiscriminatory Evaluation Process (See Figure 11–2) | |
| [Slide 11-9] Determining the Presence<br>• Usually in early childhood<br>• Often uses some of the same tests given to students with mental retardation and severe/multiple disabilities<br>• Criteria may include:<br> ▪ Speech and language<br> ▪ Academic achievement<br> ▪ Cognitive functioning<br> ▪ Medical physical status<br>• Autism Diagnostic Interview—Revised | |
| [Slide 11-10] Determining the Nature of Specially Designed Instruction and Services<br>• Functional assessment—an ecological assessment<br> ▪ Describe the nature of the behaviors<br> ▪ Gather information from interested parties<br> ▪ Determine why the student engages in problem behavior<br> ▪ Hypothesize relationship between behavior and events before, during, and after the behavior<br> ▪ Incorporate functional assessment information into the IEP<br> ▪ Help student develop alternative behaviors | |

| | |
|---|---|
| [Slide 11-11] Partnering for Special Education and Related Services<br>• Positive Behavioral Supports: Individual Support Program<br>• Questions in a functional behavioral assessment:<br>  ▪ What is the nature of the behavior?<br>  ▪ In what contexts does it occur or not occur?<br>  ▪ What are its antecedents and consequences?<br>  ▪ What are its communicative functions?<br>• Then develop a plan, to be used in all settings, that addresses:<br>  ▪ Long-term supports for the child and family<br>  ▪ Strategies to use to extinguish the child's problem behavior<br>  ▪ Strategies to replace the problem behaviors with more appropriate behaviors<br>  ▪ Consequences that teach the child that more functional skills work better | |
| [Slide 11-12] Determining Supplementary Aids and Services<br>• Address the domains of access, classroom ecology, and task modifications<br>• Access involves modifications to the community, campus, building, or classroom to ensure physical and cognitive access.<br>  ▪ Also design IEPs to provide "behavioral access"<br>  ▪ The lunchroom is a frequent environment in which problem behaviors occur; consider modifications to seating<br>  ▪ Include accommodations for before and after school and in the hall between classes<br>  ▪ Develop visual schedules | |
| [Slide 11-13] Planning for Universal Design for Learning<br>• Some characteristics associated with autism Spectrum disorders are potential areas of learning strengths and provide a basis for curriculum adaptation<br>  ▪ Ability to focus attention on detailed information<br>  ▪ May excel in areas of the curriculum that are not as language-based, such as math or science<br>• Mnemonic strategies<br>• Keyword<br>• Pegword<br>• Letter | |

| | |
|---|---|
| [Slide 11-14] Planning for Other Educational Needs<br>• Provide students instructional supports that enable them to develop and maintain friendships<br>• Promoting friendships<br>   ▪ Include students in all areas<br>   ▪ Use peer buddy programs<br>   ▪ Use person-centered planning models that involve peers<br>   ▪ Ensure peers learn about the goals of inclusion | |
| [Slide 11-15] Planning for Other Educational Needs<br>• Students' IEPs should address the following instructional areas:<br>   ▪ Trustworthiness and loyalty<br>   ▪ Conflict resolution<br>   ▪ General friendship skills<br>   ▪ Positive interaction style<br>   ▪ Taking the perspective of others | |
| [Slide 11-16] Early Childhood Students<br>• Early intervention and preschool programs use different approaches, including the following:<br>   ▪ Applied behavior analytic techniques, such as discrete trial training<br>   ▪ Incidental teaching in natural environments<br>   ▪ Communication, sensory processing, motor planning, and shared affect with caregivers and peers<br>• Social stories address the "hidden curriculum" | |
| [Slide 11-17] Elementary and Middle School Students<br>• Positive behavior supports<br>• Proactive, problem-solving, and data-based approach to improving appropriate behavior and achieving important academic, social, and communication outcomes<br>• Instruct students to replace their problem behavior with appropriate behavior<br>• Also seek to rearrange school environments and change school systems to prevent students from engaging in problem behaviors<br>• Primary goal of universal support is to create a positive learning context for all students | |

| | |
|---|---|
| [Slide 11-18] Secondary and Transition Students<br>• The techniques underlying positive behavior support emerged from a set of strategies referred to as applied behavior analysis (ABA)<br>• ABA uses the principles of operant psychology<br>• Discrete trial training is based on the "three term contingency" outlined by applied behavior analysis:<br>    ▪ Presentation of the discriminative stimulus (cue)<br>    ▪ Presentation of the prompting stimulus (if needed)<br>    ▪ The response<br>    ▪ The reinforcing stimulus | |
| [Slide 11-19] Educational Placement (See Figure 11–4) | |
| [Slide 11-20] Measuring Students' Progress<br>• Autism Screening Instrument for Educational Planning (ASIEP-2)<br>• Measures progress in addressing other educational needs<br>• Measure outcomes related to school-wide positive behavior interventions and supports<br>    ▪ Direct counts of problem behavior<br>    ▪ Problem behavior reported by environment or time of day<br>    ▪ Indirect indicators of success<br>• Data collection tools<br>    ▪ School Wide Information System<br>    ▪ School-Wide Evaluation Tool (SET)<br>    ▪ Self-Assessment of Contextual Fit in Schools | |
| [Slide 11-21] Making Accommodations for Assessment<br>• Students with autism may perform better on standardized assessments when they are provided with more frequent positive reinforcement<br>• They may also perform better when assessments are administered by a familiar person<br>    ▪ Presence of the examiner minimizes the students' anxiety and stress associated with testing | |

| | |
|---|---|
| [Slide 11-22] Looking to Jeremy's Future<br>• Plans to continue on to his local high school<br>• Possible opportunities to work with the local weather forecaster<br>• May be able to use the local bus system to get around the city and volunteer in the family church with his parents<br>• Seems likely he can become part of the neighborhood Chamber of Commerce activities<br>• He could possibly go on to attend the local community college to develop a career utilizing his strong mapping skills | |

## Activities: Applying Your Learning

Just as the textbook described Universal Design for Learning as the way for you to teach children, the principles work well for adult learners too. Rather than just taking notes, taking quizzes, and writing essays, the following activities will help you to learn the material on a deeper level and remember it better.

1. Mnemonics. Mnemonics work very well with students with Asperger syndrome. Mnemonics are sometimes even more effective if they are developed by the student or the class. There are also graphical mnemonics that can be used. You can make them up as well. Can you make up a letter mnemonic to remember the planets of the solar system? What words would make a sentence? The funnier or stranger it is, the more likely it will be remembered.

M

V

E

M

J

S

U

N

P

Graphical mnemonics are helpful too. For example, what picture can you draw for the greater than and less than symbols to make them memorable for children?

What other mnemonics do you know that have helped you to remember information? Could you make up another one that would help you in this class?

2. Social Stories. Social stories were developed by Carol Gray and are very useful for teaching social skills to students with autism. They are stories written from the child's perspective and are intended to teach social skills to students. The social stories are repeated to the student. To construct a social story, four types of sentences are included.

- **Descriptive sentences** describe the behavior steps. They include the who, what, when, where, and why of the behavior. There should be several descriptive sentences.
- **Directive sentences** direct the individual to the desired response. This is where the appropriate behavior is positively stated. Keep it brief.
- **Perspective sentences** describe the thoughts and feelings of others in the situation. It gives an outside account of how the behavior is perceived by others. There may be several perspective sentences.
- **Control sentences** are statements where the individual constructs a memory cue or mnemonic to help him or her remember the story and the desired behavior. They are not appropriate for every story or helpful to all individuals or situations. This should also be brief.

Write a social story for yourself on another piece of paper. Write it from your perspective. It should not be longer than a page. The topic should be a social skill that you have awkwardness with or avoid. An example may be asking for directions, speaking in public, or asking for help. You are welcome to illustrate the story or to use graphics. There are examples of social stories at the Companion Website at http://www.prenhall.com/turnbull.

How would this strategy be useful for teaching a student with autism?

3. Other interactive activities are available at the Companion Website found at http://www.prenhall.com/turnbull. There are informative videotapes that showcase individuals with disabilities and some of the behavioral therapies used to teach children with autism. Also, information about the vaccine debate is presented. Finally, there are several informative case study activities that showcase different behavioral methods used with students with autism.

4. Do not forget the DVD cases packaged with your textbook. There you can see video clips of the individuals discussed in the book.

Use your *Real Lives & Exceptionalities* DVD to view Jonathan, a young man with autism, participating with disabled and nondisabled peers in *Project Success*, a community service organization. Click on "Beyond School," and then select "Jonathan" (Clip 6). Do you believe Jonathan benefits from being in *Project Success*? How?

*The questions that correspond to the DVD case studies are on the DVD, but they are also found in the back of this Student Study Guide. This will allow you to see the questions ahead of time. You are also welcome to write notes or answer the questions before typing them on the DVD.*

## Practice Quiz: Assessing Your Knowledge

Below are some questions to help you review the content in the chapter. Answers to the questions are provided for you at the end of the Student Study Guide. Circle the correct answer for each question.

1. Which of the following "conditions" is similar to autism except without significant delays in language development or intellectual functioning?　　PRAXIS 1　　　　　CEC 2
   A. Savant syndrome
   B. Down syndrome
   C. Asperger syndrome
   D. Huntingtons syndrome

2. What does the "theory of the mind" attempt to explain?　PRAXIS 1　　　　　CEC 3
   A. The large differences in intellectual functioning among those with autism
   B. The reasons why individuals with autism do not develop appropriate language skills
   C. The reasons why some individuals with autism have some exceptional skills in one specific area
   D. The reasons why individuals with autism do not develop reciprocal relationships with others

3. What type of repetitive behavior is George displaying when, as he is being introduced to someone new, always says: Do you have a sister? Do you have a brother? Do you have a nephew? Do you have a niece? Do you have a . . . etc. (The list goes on and on.)　　　　PRAXIS 1　　　　　CEC 2
   A. Obsessions
   B. Tics
   C. Perseveration
   D. Echolalia

4. Which of the following students is exhibiting pica?　　PRAXIS 1　　　　　CEC 2
   A. Marcia, who eats dirt
   B. Betty, who bangs her head on the table
   C. Deanna, who sings throughout the day
   D. Wilma, who has frequent bathroom accidents

5. Which of the following is not considered a cause of autism?　　PRAXIS 1　　　　　CEC 2
   A. Genetic factors
   B. Brain abnormalities
   C. Emotionally cold parents
   D. Biochemical dysfunction

6. The prevalence rate for autism is 10 children per:　　PRAXIS 1　　　　　CEC 2
   A. 100
   B. 1,000
   C. 10,000
   D. 100,000

7. Which of the following was not listed as one of the levels or components of positive behavior support?
   　　PRAXIS 3　　　　　CEC 3
   A. Universal support
   B. Group support
   C. Teacher support
   D. Individual support

8. What intervention method has been especially helpful in teaching children with autism how to respond to cues that are part of the hidden curriculum in schools? PRAXIS 3      CEC 4
   A. Social stories
   B. Role playing activities
   C. Self-management systems
   D. Peer tutoring

9. What term do teachers sometimes use to refer to some or all five of the impairments associated with pervasive developmental disorders?      PRAXIS 1      CEC 2
   A. Autism
   B. Asperger syndrome
   C. Autism spectrum disorder
   D. Pervasive autism disorder

10. What is the intellectual functioning level of most individuals with Asperger syndrome?
         PRAXIS 1      CEC 2
    A. Well above average
    B. Above average
    C. Average
    D. Below average

11. What is the goal of a functional assessment?      PRAXIS 3      CEC 8
    A. To determine IEP goals and objectives related to functional daily living skills
    B. To evaluate the child's ability to complete everyday tasks such as eating, feeding, and toileting
    C. To identify relationships between the behavior and events that trigger it
    D. To help the child develop self-monitoring skills

12. Which of the following would be the least preferred action to take if Cindy, a student with autism, learned very slowly and needed much more time to acquire even simple concepts?      PRAXIS 3      CEC 3
    A. Use visual images to teach the concept
    B. Make the requirement less structured
    C. Use music to teach abstract concepts
    D. Involve peers

13. Which 2 disabilities does the Autism Diagnostic Interview—Revised differentiate? PRAXIS 1      CEC 8
    A. It differentiates between those with autism and those with Asperger syndrome.
    B. It differentiates between those with autism and those with a communication disorder.
    C. It differentiates between those with autism and those with mental retardation.
    D. It differentiates between those with autism and those with an emotional/behavioral disorder.

14. An effective curriculum adaptation for students with autism is:      PRAXIS 3      CEC 4
    A. Indirect instruction
    B. Cooperative learning
    C. Mnemonic strategies
    D. Mastery learning

15. One way that teachers and administrators can help students with autism reduce their anxiety on test days is to:
         PRAXIS 3      CEC 10
    A. Allow them not to be assessed
    B. Provide a familiar examiner
    C. Provide other accommodations not specified
    D. Provide extra snacks

Now that you have completed your chapter study, go back to the chapter objectives and see if you have truly met them. You may want to write out your responses to the chapter objectives so that you can check your understanding against the chapter outline or the text.

# Chapter 12: Understanding Students with Physical Disabilities and Other Health Impairments

## Objectives: Guiding Your Chapter Reading

The content in this chapter is presented to help you achieve the following objectives. Once you complete your study of the chapter, see if you can do what the objectives describe. If not, you may need to do some more reviewing of the chapter and your class notes.

- Define and identify the characteristics of students with physical disabilities and other health impairments
- Recall the major causes of physical disabilities and other health impairments
- Explain the assessment and evaluation practices for students with physical disabilities and other health impairments
- Identify the major issues impacting students with physical disabilities and other health impairments
- Describe successful instructional practices and accommodations for students with physical disabilities and other health impairments

## Standards Matrices: Relating Content to Professional Standards

The matrices, or charts, below help you see how the professional standards from the Council for Exceptional Children (CEC) and PRAXIS™ apply to the content in this chapter. In addition, you can refer to the margin notes throughout the chapter and the activities at the end of each chapter to make sure you understand how these standards apply to the content in the field of special education. These standards are important for you to know because they provide the basis for the professional teacher certification examinations and content covered in these exams.

| CEC Standards | Chapter Topic |
| --- | --- |
| 1 | • IDEA<br>• Definition of physical disabilities<br>• Definition of other health impairments |
| 2 | • Case study<br>• Characteristics of physical disabilities as they relate to cerebral palsy and spina bifida<br>• Causes of physical disabilities as they relate to cerebral palsy and spina bifida<br>• Characteristics of other health impairments as they relate to epilepsy and asthma<br>• Causes of other health impairments as they relate to epilepsy and asthma |
| 3 | • Differences in intellectual functioning<br>• Supplementary aids and services<br>• Universal design<br>• Testing accommodations |
| 4 | • Universal design<br>• Effective strategies as they relate to early childhood, middle school, and high school years |
| 5 | • Planning for other educational needs<br>• Promoting friendships<br>• Inclusion |
| 6 | |
| 7 | • Supplementary aids and services<br>• National Instructional Materials Accessibility Standard<br>• Inclusion<br>• Token system |
| 8 | • Evaluation and assessment<br>• Functional behavioral assessment<br>• Measuring student progress |
| 9 | • Characteristics of physical disabilities as they relate to cerebral palsy and spina bifida |

| | • Characteristics of other health impairments as they relate to epilepsy and asthma |
|---|---|
| | • Partnering for special education and related services |
| 10 | • Case study |
| | • Partnering for special education and related services |
| | • Planning for other educational needs |
| | • Inclusion |

| PRAXIS™ Standards | Chapter Topic |
|---|---|
| 1 | • Case study |
| | • Characteristics of physical disabilities as they relate to cerebral palsy and spina bifida |
| | • Characteristics of other health impairments as they relate to epilepsy and asthma |
| | • Causes of physical disabilities as they relate to cerebral palsy and spina bifida |
| | • Causes of other health impairments as they relate to epilepsy and asthma |
| 2 | • IDEA |
| | • Definitions of physical disabilities and other health impairments |
| 3 | • Partnering for special education and related services |
| | • Supplementary aids and services |
| | • Universal design |
| | • Testing accommodations |
| | • Evaluation and assessment |
| | • Measuring student progress |
| | • Planning for other educational needs |
| | • Inclusion |

## Checking for Understanding: Key Terms

To check that you understand the basic terms and vocabulary in the chapter, use the space provided to write the definitions or descriptions in your own words. Then, check the chapter to see how accurate your definition is, making sure you understand the context, or situation, in which the word is used. Reviewing these terms will help you better understand the concepts that support the content in this chapter.

| Term | Definition/Description | (✓) |
|---|---|---|
| cerebral palsy | | |
| spastic | | |
| athetoid | | |
| ataxic | | |

| | | |
|---|---|---|
| mixed | | |
| topological classification system | | |
| monoplegia | | |
| paraplegia | | |
| hemiplegia | | |
| triplegia | | |
| quadriplegia | | |
| diplegia | | |
| double hemiplegia | | |
| prenatal causes | | |
| perimatal causes | | |
| postnatal causes | | |
| spina bifida | | |

| | | |
|---|---|---|
| spina bifida occulta | | |
| meningocele | | |
| myelomeningocele | | |
| lumbar nerves | | |
| sacral nerves | | |
| clean intermittent catheterization | | |
| primarily altered consciousness | | |
| absence seizures | | |
| tonic-clonic seizures | | |
| partial seizures | | |
| neuroimaging | | |
| material serum-alpha-fetal protein | | |
| pneumatic or puffing switches | | |

## Chapter Outline: Taking Chapter Notes

The following outline is taken from the PowerPoint slides or overheads that your professor uses in class for this chapter. In the slides, there are several embedded links to more information for this chapter. Please go to the Companion Website at http://www.prenhall.com/turnbull to access them easily.

If you take your Student Study Guide to class, you can use this outline for taking notes on the chapter or for review. It will also allow you to listen to lectures and participate in class discussions without having to copy down all the PowerPoint information.

The notes below are set up for recording information from the chapter in a particular way—an adapted Cornell method of taking notes. In this adapted Cornell method, you underline, or highlight, information presented to you. In addition to highlighting, you can write information or explanations on the left-hand side of the table. Soon after the class presentation or reading the chapter, rewrite the notes from the left-hand side in your own words, using key terms and phrases. To study for quizzes or exams, you can cover up the left-hand side and use the right-hand side of the table to cue yourself about the information.

You also may just jot notes on the right-hand side to help you. Since this outline reduces the chapter for you, it will be a useful study aid. The summary at the end of the chapter is another useful resource to use for review.

| Chapter 12<br>Understanding Students with Physical Disabilities and Other Health Impairments | NOTES |
|---|---|
| [Slide 12-1] Chapter 12 Objectives: At the end of this chapter you should be able to:<br>• Define and identify the characteristics of students with physical disabilities and other health impairments<br>• Recall the major causes of physical disabilities and other health impairments<br>• Explain the assessment and evaluation practices for students with physical disabilities and other health impairments<br>• Identify the major issues impacting students with physical disabilities and other health impairments<br>• Describe successful instructional practices and accommodations for students with physical disabilities and other health impairments | |

| | |
|---|---|
| **[Slide 12-2] Who Is Ryan Frisella? Who Is Kwashon Drayton?**<br>• Ryan is an eighth-grade student in a gifted and talented program<br>• He has a lot of hobbies, including riding a hand bike, playing soccer, and being involved in drama<br>• Ryan also has cerebral palsy<br>• He uses a walker and a wheelchair and can pull himself to a standing position<br>• His family has always held great expectations for Ryan<br>• Kwashon is a nine-year-old fourth grader<br>• He has asthma, just like his mother, grandmother, and great-grandmother<br>• He takes four medications a day for his asthma<br>• He now plays basketball and plans to play football, but is unable to participate in track<br>• He has allergies and must avoid certain irritants, such as dust, pollen, and grass<br>• He does not have an IEP for his asthma, but has a 504 plan | |
| **[Slide 12-3] Defining Physical Disabilities**<br>• IDEA uses the term *orthopedic impairments*, but educators typically use the term *physical disabilities*.<br>• Typically refers to a large group of students who are very different from each other<br>• The term may be used to also include students with:<br>  ▪ Severe and multiple disabilities<br>  ▪ Other health impairments<br>  ▪ Traumatic brain injury<br>• Focus on two types of physical disabilities:<br>  ▪ Cerebral palsy<br>  ▪ Spina bifida | |
| **[Slide 12-4] Characteristics of Cerebral Palsy**<br>• A disorder of movement or posture due to damage in the brain<br>• Four types<br>  ▪ Spastic<br>  ▪ Athetoid<br>  ▪ Ataxic<br>  ▪ Mixed<br>• Causes<br>  ▪ Prenatal<br>  ▪ Perinatal<br>  ▪ Postnatal<br>• Other associated conditions<br>  ▪ Possible mental retardation<br>  ▪ Speech and communication problems | |

| | |
|---|---|
| [Slide 12-5] Characteristics of Spina Bifida<br>• Malformation of the spinal cord<br>• Three common forms<br>   ▪ Spina bifida occulta<br>   ▪ Meningocele<br>   ▪ Myelomeningocele<br>• Causes<br>   ▪ Occurs in early pregnancy<br>• Mothers using regular supplements containing folic acid reduce their risk<br>• Other associated conditions<br>   ▪ Usually does not affect intelligence<br>   ▪ Depending on location of defect, may cause incontinence or other urinary and bowel problems | |
| [Slide 12-6] Defining Other Health Impairments<br>• IDEA defines as chronic health problems those that have an adverse impact on educational performance.<br>• Distinguished from severe and multiple disabilities, physical disabilities, and traumatic brain injuries<br>• May be:<br>   ▪ Chronic: develops slowly and has long-lasting symptoms<br>   ▪ Acute: develops quickly with intense symptoms that last a relatively short period of time | |
| [Slide 12-7] Prevalence of Other Health Impairments<br>• In 2003–2004, 452,045 students (0.7% of the school-age population) ages 6 to 21 served under IDEA<br>• Of all students, 10–30% will experience a childhood chronic illness lasting three months or longer<br>• More than 200 specific health impairments exist | |
| [Slide 12-8] Characteristics of Epilepsy<br>• Characterized by seizures (abnormal electrical discharges in the brain)<br>   ▪ Generalized seizures<br>      • Tonic-clonic<br>      • Absence<br>   ▪ Partial seizures<br>      • Temporal lobe, also known as psychomotor<br>      • Focal motor or focal sensory<br>      • Myoclonic<br>• Teachers can help by:<br>   ▪ Identifying and eliminating environmental factors that trigger seizures<br>   ▪ Provide classmates with factual | |

| | |
|---|---|
| information on seizures | |
| [Slide 12-9] Characteristics of Epilepsy<br>• Conditions associated with epilepsy<br>    ▪ Most children have average IQs;<br>     however, children with epilepsy are<br>     more likely to have learning disabilities<br>    ▪ They are at risk for being diagnosed with<br>     ADHD<br>    ▪ Adolescents with epilepsy are reported<br>     to have higher levels of depression<br>• Causes<br>    ▪ Insults to the brain create a level of brain<br>     vulnerability that can result in the onset<br>     of seizures<br>        • Prenatal (infections), perinatal<br>         (birth trauma), and postnatal<br>         (poisoning, stress, fatigue, sleep<br>         deprivation)<br>    ▪ In three-fourths of individuals with<br>     epilepsy, the cause is unknown<br>• Prevalence<br>    ▪ Up to 10% of all children experience a<br>     seizure at some point in their childhood<br>     or youth; only 1% of the population has<br>     epilepsy by the age of 20 | |
| [Slide 12-10] Characteristics of Asthma<br>• Most prevalent chronic illness of children and<br>  leading cause of school absences<br>• Prevalence has become epidemic, increasing by<br>  72% from 1982 to 1994<br>• Symptoms can vary widely<br>    ▪ Mild intermittent<br>    ▪ Mild persistent<br>    ▪ Moderate persistent<br>    ▪ Severe persistent<br>• Students may use anti-inflammatories or<br>  bronchodilators<br>• Teachers can help by:<br>    ▪ Following students' leads about exercise<br>     regimens<br>    ▪ Knowing essential first-aid skills for<br>     managing asthma episodes<br>    ▪ Following a student's action plan for<br>     episodes | |

| | |
|---|---|
| [Slide 12-11] Characteristics of Asthma<br>• Conditions associated with asthma<br>    ▪ Fatigue from waking during the night because of breathing difficulties<br>    ▪ Absences from school due to symptoms<br>    ▪ Fatigue and school absenteeism is associated with lower academic performance<br>• Causes<br>    ▪ Asthma symptoms are triggered by food, exercise, cold air, respiratory infections, and environmental allergens, including cigarette smoke, dust, mold, gases, and chemicals<br>    ▪ Sometimes asthma is an inherited condition<br>• Prevalence<br>    ▪ Approximately 7–10% of the general childhood population has a diagnosis of asthma<br>    ▪ The risk of asthma increases among students from diverse backgrounds | |
| [Slide 12-12] Nondiscriminatory Evaluation Process (See Figure 12–5) | |
| [Slide 12-13] Nondiscriminatory Evaluation Process (See Figure 12–6) | |
| [Slide 12-14] Determining the Presence<br>• Neuroimaging<br>• Prenatal screening<br>    ▪ Maternal serum alpha-fetoprotein<br>    ▪ Fetal surgery | |
| [Slide 12-15] Partnering for Special Education and Related Services<br>• Health condition must adversely impact educational performance for an IEP<br>• Otherwise, develop a 504 plan<br>• Importance of school nurse on the team<br>• Components of the health care plan<br>• Related services may also include school health care services provided by medical personnel<br>• IEPs may also contain respite care for family members | |
| [Slide 12-16] Determining the Nature of Specially Designed Instruction and Services<br>• Physical and occupational therapists conduct evaluation<br>• School Function Assessment<br>    • Participation<br>    • Task Supports<br>    • Activity Performance | |

| | |
|---|---|
| [Slide 12-17] Determining Supplementary Aids and Services<br>• Adaptive Switches (See Figure 12–8)<br>   ▪ Pressure<br>   ▪ Timed<br>   ▪ Pneumatic or puffing switches<br>   ▪ Movements<br>   ▪ Sound<br>• Electronic Wheelchairs (See Technology Tips, p. 301)<br>   ▪ Transporting the chair<br>   ▪ Adjusting the size<br>   ▪ Recharging the batteries<br>   ▪ Selecting the navigation tools<br>   ▪ Assuring safety | |
| [Slide 12-18] Planning for Universal Design for Learning<br>• Electronic text<br>• NIMAS<br>   ▪ Digital files can be "read" by commercially available media players that allow information in the source file to be presented in multiple ways<br>   ▪ Thinking Reader | |
| [Slide 12-19] Planning for Other Educational Needs<br>• Adaptive PE<br>• Allows for student with disabilities to participate in a typical sport or physical activity<br>• Modified equipment<br>   ▪ Beeping ball for student with visual impairment | |
| [Slide 12-20] Early Childhood Students<br>• Token economies<br>   ▪ Not age- or disability-specific<br>   ▪ Relates to errorless learning and using prompts for modifying the "three-term contingency" sequence (discriminative stimulus, response, and reinforcing stimulus)<br>• Another way to modify the three-term contingency is by changing aspects of the reinforcing stimulus (e.g., altering the schedule on which a reinforcer is delivered)<br>   ▪ Token economies use reinforcers | |

| | |
|---|---|
| [Slide 12-21] Elementary and Middle School Students<br>• Self-awareness<br>    ▪ Middle school is difficult for most children, and a disability or illness only adds to the stress<br>    ▪ The term *self-awareness* refers to one's understanding of oneself as a unique individual and is often used in conjunction with the notions of self-understanding and self-knowledge<br>    ▪ This includes the process referred to as disability awareness, which involves the capacity of an individual to appraise his or her own abilities as a function of a specific disabling condition | |
| [Slide 12-22] Secondary and Transition Students<br>• Driver's Ed<br>    ▪ A driver's license is the key to freedom and independence<br>    ▪ Having a driver's license impacts a student's social activity<br>    ▪ Schools need modified vehicles for students with disabilities | |
| [Slide 12-23] Educational Placement of Students with Physical Disabilities (See Figure 12–10) | |
| [Slide 12-24] Educational Placement of Students with Other Health Impairments (See Figure 12–11) | |
| [Slide 12-25] Measuring Students' Progress<br>• Using Computers for Curriculum-Based Measurement<br>• Measurement in Adaptive Physical Education<br>    ▪ Cardiovascular function<br>    ▪ Body composition<br>    ▪ Muscle strength and endurance<br>    ▪ Muscle and joint flexibility<br>    ▪ Posture evaluation<br>    ▪ Mobility | |
| [Slide 12-26] Making Accommodations for Assessment<br>• Computer-based assessment<br>• Frequent breaks<br>• Scribe<br>• Physical access to testing environment<br>• Security concerns, test materials, and environmental controls | |

| [Slide 12-27] Looking to Ryan's and Kwashon's Future | |
|---|---|
| • Ryan may attend college<br>• Perhaps Ryan will become involved in drama, and eventually become an actor<br>• Both boys have unlimited options<br>• Kwashon may go to college and pursue majors in any of his interests: sports administration, health, education<br>• Kwashon may follow his interests into the medical field<br>• Perhaps Kwashon will be a doctor in sports medicine, or maybe a pulmonary specialist, working with other children who share his illness | |

## Activities: Applying Your Learning

Just as the textbook described Universal Design for Learning as the way for you to teach children, the principles work well for adult learners too. Rather than just taking notes, taking quizzes, and writing essays, the following activities will help you to learn the material on a deeper level and remember it better.

1. Health care intervention. The textbook discusses when you should seek help if a child has an epileptic seizure or an asthma attack, but that is easier said than done if you are the sole teacher of 30 students. What kinds of arrangements can you make beforehand to make sure you can get assistance for the student and make sure your students are supervised? Write down the steps you will follow in a health emergency situation in your classroom.

2. Wheelchair etiquette. Many people are not familiar with talking to people in wheelchairs and often make mistakes without realizing it. Take the following quiz to see how familiar you are with wheelchair etiquette.

**True or False**
A. Touching a person's wheelchair is almost always acceptable.

B. Make sure not to reach out your hand to shake the person's hand; they may have physical limitations.

C. Rarely speak to the person in the wheelchair; focus on the person assisting him or her.

D. Never use expressions such as "Let's go for a walk."

E. Pat the person on his or her head; it is a sign of affection.

F. Do not sit down when talking to a person in a wheelchair.

The answers are at http://www.wheelchairnet.org/WCN_TownHall/Docs/etiquette.html

3. Other interactive activities are available at the Companion Website found at http://www.prenhall.com/turnbull. There are videos of individuals with physical disabilities and health impairments. See the examples of successful inclusion. There is a lot more information about specific physical disabilities and health impairments. The issue of children dying is also addressed in one activity.

4. Do not forget the DVD cases packaged with your textbook. There you can see video clips of the individuals discussed in the book.

Use your *Real Lives & Exceptionalities* DVD to see what it is like living with cerebral palsy. Click on "Beyond School" and view "Maxine" (Clip 3). Do you believe Maxine has accomplished so much despite her disability or because of her disability?

Use your *Real Lives & Exceptionalities* DVD to critically think about working with Ryan under "Questions," located below "Meet Ryan." Would you like to have Ryan as a student? Why or why not?

*The questions that correspond to the DVD case studies are on the DVD, but they are also found in the back of this Student Study Guide. This will allow you to see the questions ahead of time. You are also welcome to write notes or answer the questions before typing them on the DVD.*

## Practice Quiz: Assessing Your Knowledge

Below are some questions to help you review the content in the chapter. Answers to the questions are provided for you at the end of the Student Study Guide. Circle the correct answer for each question.

1.  Which type of cerebral palsy accounts for about 70–80% of all individuals with this condition?
    PRAXIS 1        CEC 2
    A. Spastic
    B. Athetoid
    C. Ataxic
    D. Mixed

2.  What does the topographical classification system for cerebral palsy consider?     PRAXIS 1     CEC 2
    A. The level of intellectual impairment involved
    B. The nature of the person's movement
    C. The body part(s) that is/are affected
    D. The age of onset

3.  Which of these is a perinatal cause of a physical disability?     PRAXIS 1     CEC 2
    A. Infection before birth
    B. Lack of oxygen during birth
    C. Brain injury after birth
    D. Epilepsy

4.  Which one of the following was not mentioned as a "more typical" (or prevalent) condition associated with the other health impairments category?     PRAXIS 1     CEC 2
    A. Sickle cell disease
    B. Human immunodeficiency virus
    C. Tourettes syndrome
    D. Cancer

5.  Which condition has an unknown cause but is believed to occur during the very early days of pregnancy?
    PRAXIS 1        CEC 2
    A. Spina bifida
    B. Cerebral palsy
    C. Muscular dystrophy
    D. Amputations

6.  Marie is described as having monoplegia. What does this mean?     PRAXIS 1     CEC 2
    A. One half of her body is affected by her disability.
    B. One limb is affected by her disability.
    C. One body organ is affected by her disability.
    D. One upper limb and one lower limb are affected by her disability.

7.  What is the purpose of scooters, walkers, crutches, and bicycles?     PRAXIS 1     CEC 2
    A. Positioning
    B. Mobility
    C. Isolated support
    D. Sensory support

8.  When promoting self-awareness in students:     PRAXIS 3     CEC 4
    A. Do not regard self-awareness as consisting only of the acceptance of a limitation.
    B. Protect students who may engage in risky behavior, especially during adolescence.
    C. Make sure students are realistic and know their limitations.
    D. Sometimes it is better for students to not be truly aware of themselves.

9. Generally speaking, how do students with physical disabilities compare to those without disabilities on indicators relating to transitional and postsecondary adjustments?   PRAXIS 3          CEC 5
   A. They faired slightly better than their nondisabled peers.
   B. They faired as well as their nondisabled peers.
   C. They faired slightly below their nondisabled peers.
   D. They faired well below their nondisabled peers.

10. Which professional on the IEP team is concerned with the student's fine motor skills?
            PRAXIS 3               CEC 10
    A. Physical therapist
    B. Occupational therapist
    C. Adaptive PE teacher
    D. Assistive technology specialist

11. Which of the following students experienced a tonic-clonic seizure?        PRAXIS 1        CEC 2
    A. During her seizure, Shirley picked at her clothes.
    B. During his seizure, Ronnie appeared to be in a dreamlike state.
    C. During his seizure, George had a convulsion.
    D. During his seizure, Bill imagined things that were not really occurring.

12. What term refers to the unusual sensation that may occur right before a seizure?        PRAXIS 1        CEC 2
    A. Hemoglobin
    B. Automatism
    C. Convulsion
    D. Aura

13. Which of the following is a misconception about children with asthma?        PRAXIS 1        CEC 2
    A. Triggers for an attack are dust, chalk, mold, pollen
    B. Children have trouble inhaling
    C. Children must use their medication as soon as they experience symptoms
    D. Moderate exercise is good

14. The specific body location of the movement impairment that correlates with the location of the brain damage is called:        PRAXIS 3               CEC 1
    A. Phylum classification system
    B. Topographical classification system
    C. Classification system
    D. Physiological classification system

15. What is the specific name of the child's plan that specifies procedures and standards for taking naps, administering medication, and making up work during absences?   PRAXIS 3               CEC 1
    A. Health accommodation plan
    B. Emergency plan
    C. Health care plan
    D. Health impairment plan

Now that you have completed your chapter study, go back to the chapter objectives and see if you have truly met them. You may want to write out your responses to the chapter objectives so that you can check your understanding against the chapter outline or the text.

# Chapter 13: Understanding Students with Traumatic Brain Injury

## Objectives: Guiding Your Chapter Reading
The content in this chapter is presented to help you achieve the following objectives. Once you complete your study of the chapter, see if you can do what the objectives describe. If not, you may need to do some more reviewing of the chapter and your class notes.

- Define and identify the characteristics of students with traumatic brain injury
- Recall the major causes of traumatic brain injury
- Explain the assessment and evaluation practices for students with traumatic brain injury
- Identify the major issues impacting students with traumatic brain injury
- Describe successful instructional practices and accommodations for students with traumatic brain injury

## Standards Matrices: Relating Content to Professional Standards
The matrices, or charts, below help you see how the professional standards from the Council for Exceptional Children (CEC) and PRAXIS™ apply to the content in this chapter. In addition, you can refer to the margin notes throughout the chapter and the activities at the end of each chapter to make sure you understand how these standards apply to the content in the field of special education. These standards are important for you to know because they provide the basis for the professional teacher certification examinations and content covered in these exams.

| CEC Standards | Chapter Topic |
|---|---|
| 1 | • IDEA<br>• Definition of traumatic brain injury |
| 2 | • Case study<br>• Characteristics of traumatic brain injury<br>• Causes of traumatic brain injury |
| 3 | • Supplementary aids and services<br>• Universal design<br>• Testing accommodations |
| 4 | • Cognitive retraining<br>• Universal design<br>• Effective strategies as they relate to early childhood, middle, and high school years<br>• Collaborative teaming<br>• Cooperative learning |
| 5 | • Planning for other educational needs<br>• Cooperative learning<br>• Inclusion |
| 6 | |
| 7 | • Supplementary aids and services<br>• Virtual assistant software<br>• Inclusion<br>• Collaborative teaming<br>• Cooperative learning<br>• Problem solving and decision-making instruction<br>• Transition |
| 8 | • Evaluation and assessment<br>• Functional behavioral assessment<br>• Measuring student progress |
| 9 | • Characteristics of traumatic brain injury<br>• Partnering for special education and related services |
| 10 | • Case study |

| | • Partnering for special education and related services |
| | • Planning for other educational needs |
| | • Inclusion |
| | • Collaborative teaming |
| | • Transition |

| PRAXIS™ Standards | Chapter Topic |
|---|---|
| 1 | • Case study<br>• Characteristics of traumatic brain injury<br>• Causes of traumatic brain injury |
| 2 | • IDEA<br>• Definitions of traumatic brain injury |
| 3 | • Partnering for special education and related services<br>• Supplementary aids and services<br>• Universal design<br>• Testing accommodations<br>• Evaluation and assessment<br>• Measuring student progress<br>• Planning for other educational needs<br>• Inclusion |

## Checking for Understanding: Key Terms

To check that you understand the basic terms and vocabulary in the chapter, use the space provided to write the definitions or descriptions in your own words. Then, check the chapter to see how accurate your definition is, making sure you understand the context, or situation, in which the word is used. Reviewing these terms will help you better understand the concepts that support the content in this chapter.

| Term | Definition/Description | (✓) |
|---|---|---|
| traumatic brain injury | | |
| acquired injury | | |
| congenital | | |
| encephalitis | | |
| open head injury | | |

163

| | | |
|---|---|---|
| closed head injury | | |
| coma | | |
| ataxia/tremor | | |
| atrophy | | |
| central auditory processing | | |
| computerized tomography (CT) | | |
| computerized axial tomography (CAT) | | |
| magnetic resonance imaging (MRI) | | |
| functional MRI | | |
| position emission tomography (PET) | | |
| cognitive retraining | | |

## Chapter Outline: Taking Chapter Notes

The following outline is taken from the PowerPoint slides or overheads that your professor uses in class for this chapter. In the slides, there are several embedded links to more information for this chapter. Please go to the Companion Website at http://www.prenhall.com/turnbull to access them easily.

If you take your Student Study Guide to class, you can use this outline for taking notes on the chapter or for review. It will also allow you to listen to lectures and participate in class discussions without having to copy down all the PowerPoint information.

The notes below are set up for recording information from the chapter in a particular way—an adapted Cornell method of taking notes. In this adapted Cornell method, you underline, or highlight, information presented to you. In addition to highlighting, you can write information or explanations on the left-hand side of the table. Soon after the class presentation or reading the chapter, rewrite the notes from the left-hand side in your own words, using key terms and phrases. To study for quizzes or exams, you can cover up the left-hand side and use the right-hand side of the table to cue yourself about the information.

You also may just jot notes on the right-hand side to help you. Since this outline reduces the chapter for you, it will be a useful study aid. The summary at the end of the chapter is another useful resource to use for review.

| Chapter 13<br>Understanding Students with Traumatic Brain Injury | NOTES |
|---|---|
| [Slide 13-1] Chapter 13 Objectives: At the end of this chapter you should be able to:<br>• Define and identify the characteristics of students with traumatic brain injury<br>• Recall the major causes of traumatic brain injury<br>• Explain the assessment and evaluation practices for students with traumatic brain injury<br>• Identify the major issues impacting students with traumatic brain injury<br>• Describe successful instructional practices and accommodations for students with traumatic brain injury | |
| [Slide 13-2] Who Is Jarris Garner?<br>• Jarris is a 10-year-old girl who was involved in a serious car accident when she was only seven months old.<br>• Jarris spent much of her recovery at her grandmother's home, so she could be in quiet surroundings.<br>• Her mother had her enrolled in the Language Acquisition Program in order to focus on her use of language and communication, even learning sign language (ASL).<br>• Her entire family learned ASL in order to communicate with her, and Jarris learned how to be part of a social community.<br>• She is currently in a general education classroom; she enjoys sports but has to avoid contact sports to avoid reinjuring herself. | |
| [Slide 13-3] Defining Traumatic Brain Injury<br>• Traumatic brain injury (TBI) is an acquired injury caused by external physical force<br>• Two types of TBI:<br>　■ Closed head injury<br>　■ Open head injury<br>• Does not include congenital, infections, degenerative, or birth trauma | |

| | |
|---|---|
| [Slide 13-4] Prevalence of TBI<br>• In the 1999–2000 school year, 22,509 students (3%)<br>• Other prevalence data indicate the effects of TBI<br>    ▪ Emergency department visits, hospitalizations, and deaths<br>    ▪ About 75% of individuals who have TBI have a mild TBI<br>    ▪ Males are approximately twice as likely to sustain a TBI as females | |
| [Slide 13-5] Characteristics<br>• Characteristics will vary according to:<br>    ▪ Site and extent of injury<br>    ▪ Length of time student was in a coma<br>    ▪ Student's maturational stage at the time of injury<br>• Possible changes due to TBI:<br>    ▪ Physical<br>    ▪ Cognitive<br>    ▪ Linguistic<br>    ▪ Behavioral, emotional, and social | |
| [Slide 13-6] Determining the Causes<br>• Accidents<br>    ▪ Most are motor vehicle<br>• Falls<br>• Violence-related incidents<br>    ▪ Firearm (two-thirds are suicide attempts)<br>    ▪ Child abuse<br>• Shaken-baby syndrome<br>• Sports and recreational injuries | |
| [Slide 13-7] Nondiscriminatory Evaluation Process (See Figure 13–4) | |
| [Slide 13-8] Determining the Presence<br>• Comprehensive educational evaluation usually occurs simultaneously with medical evaluations<br>• Medical imaging:<br>    ▪ Computerized tomography (CT)<br>    ▪ Magnetic resonance imaging (MRI)<br>    ▪ Functional magnetic resonance imaging (fMRI)<br>    ▪ Positron emission tomography (PET) | |

| | |
|---|---|
| [Slide 13-9] Determining the Presence<br>• Test of Problem Solving—Elementary—analyzes a student's strengths and weaknesses:<br>    ▪ solving problems<br>    ▪ determining solutions<br>    ▪ drawing emphasis<br>    ▪ empathizing<br>    ▪ predicting outcomes<br>    ▪ using context clues<br>    ▪ comprehending vocabulary<br>• Teachers use the results of neuro-psychological testing for cognitive retraining | |
| [Slide 13-10] Determining the Nature of Specially Designed Instruction and Services<br>• Students with TBI need frequent evaluation and re-evaluation<br>• Classroom observation checklists (See Figure 13–5)<br>    ▪ Memory<br>    ▪ Attention and Concentration<br>    ▪ Executive Functioning<br>    ▪ Self-Awareness<br>    ▪ Language | |
| [Slide 13-11] Partnering for Special Education and Related Services<br>• For successful hospital to school transitions:<br>    ▪ Involve educators during hospital stay<br>    ▪ Keep school personnel updated on student medical progress<br>    ▪ Make the time for homebound instruction as short as possible<br>    ▪ Frequently monitor the student's progress after reentry<br>    ▪ Assign someone to be the point person for coordinating the transition | |
| [Slide 13-12] Determining Supplementary Aids and Services<br>• Teaching memory aids, including:<br>    ▪ Following a routine schedule<br>    ▪ Keeping appointments that are not routine<br>    ▪ Taking medications<br>    ▪ Remembering to perform a new task<br>    ▪ Marking when to start or end a task<br>• Using technology: visual assistants, PDAs, pagers/digital beepers, electronic watches | |
| [Slide 13-13] Planning for Universal Design for Learning<br>• Instructional Pacing<br>    ▪ Appropriate instructional pacing<br>    ▪ Frequent student responses<br>    ▪ Adequate processing time<br>    ▪ Monitoring responses<br>    ▪ Frequent feedback | |

| | |
|---|---|
| [Slide 13-14] Planning for Other Educational Needs<br>• Self-management<br>• Learning<br>• Thinking<br>• Problem-solving<br>• Especially when transitioning from school to adulthood | |
| [Slide 13-15] Early Childhood Students<br>• Collaborative teaming<br>   ▪ Partner to achieve a shared goal<br>   ▪ Believe that all team members have unique and needed expertise and skills, and value each person's contribution<br>   ▪ Distribute leadership throughout the team<br>• Five components of collaborative teaming<br>   ▪ Building team structure<br>   ▪ Learning teamwork skills<br>   ▪ Taking team action<br>   ▪ Teaching collaboratively<br>   ▪ Improving communication and handling conflict | |
| [Slide 13-16] Elementary and Middle School Students<br>• Cooperative learning strategies<br>• Positive interdependence<br>• Individual accountability<br>• Several ways to structure cooperative learning groups for group success<br>   ▪ Group size<br>   ▪ Detailing each student's individual task<br>   ▪ Peers holding one another accountable | |
| [Slide 13-17] Secondary and Transition Students<br>• Problem-solving<br>   ▪ Problem identification<br>   ▪ Problem explication or definition<br>   ▪ Solution generation<br>• Decision Making<br>   ▪ Identify relevant alternatives or options<br>   ▪ Identify consequences of alternatives<br>   ▪ Identify probability of each consequence<br>   ▪ Determine the value placed on each value or alternative<br>   ▪ Integrate values and consequences to select preferred option | |
| [Slide 13-18] Educational Placement (See Figure 13–6) | |

| | |
|---|---|
| [Slide 13-19] Measuring Students' Progress<br>• Analytical rubrics<br>    ▪ Link directly to specific content and student achievement standards.<br>    ▪ Focus on only one dimension of student performance (i.e., legibility versus content knowledge).<br>    ▪ There should be enough points in the scale to adequately judge performance, but not so many as to confuse the issue.<br>    ▪ Focus on specific outcomes rather than a process.<br>    ▪ Provide students with information about the rubrics and examples of high-quality performance. | |
| [Slide 13-20] Measuring Students' Progress<br>• Progress in addressing other educational needs<br>    ▪ Perceptual-motor skills coordinate visual and sensory input with motor activities<br>    ▪ Bender-Gestalt Visual Motor<br>    ▪ Collaborations with other professionals<br>• Making accommodations for assessment<br>    ▪ Test item construction<br>    ▪ The use of a scribe | |
| [Slide 13-21] Looking to Jarris's Future<br>• Jarris has mastered ASL and can communicate effectively with her family, teachers, and schoolmates.<br>• Jarris's parents want her to be able to choose and pursue whatever dreams she has.<br>• They believe she has the potential to succeed, and they believe this developed from her early involvement with the LAP. | |

## Activities: Applying Your Learning

Just as the textbook described Universal Design for Learning as the way for you to teach children, the principles work well for adult learners too. Rather than just taking notes, taking quizzes, and writing essays, the following activities will help you to learn the material on a deeper level and remember it better.

1. Classroom observation checklist. The classroom observation checklist for students with TBI gives a good description of the kinds of characteristics they exhibit. Compare and contrast the major functional domains of TBI with two other cognitive disabilities, mental retardation and learning disabilities.

| Functional Domain | Traumatic Brain Injury | Mental Retardation | Learning Disabilities |
| --- | --- | --- | --- |
| Memory | | | |
| Attention and Concentration | | | |
| Executive Functioning | | | |
| Self-Awareness | | | |
| Language | | | |

2. Problem solving. Problem solving is an important skill for all individuals, but the instructor may need to provide explicit instruction for students with TBI. Use the steps outlined in the chapter to solve one of your own problems.

Problem identification:

Problem definition or explanation:

Solution generation (fill out chart):

| Options List | Options Consequences | Option Consequence Probability | Option Value |
|---|---|---|---|
| | | | |

After filling out the chart, is it easier to decide which option to choose?

Note: If your first choice option does not work out, it is always nice to have alternatives to solve your problem!

3. Other interactive activities are available at the Companion Website found at http://www.prenhall.com/turnbull. There are several personal stories of head injury survivors. Also there are links to discussion of how the family adapts to the changes that result from having a child with TBI. Since TBI is sometimes a preventable disability, we have included links on how to prevent TBI. These links include safety activities you can do with your students.

4. Do not forget the DVD cases packaged with your textbook. There you can see video clips of the individuals discussed in the book.

Use your *Real Lives & Exceptionalities* DVD to view Jamie, who is involved in a cooperative activity. Click on "Beyond School," and then select "Jamie" (Clip 5). What characteristics of successful cooperative learning groups can you identify in this clip?

*The questions that correspond to the DVD case studies are on the DVD, but they are also found in the back of this Student Study Guide. This will allow you to see the questions ahead of time. You are also welcome to write notes or answer the questions before typing them on the DVD.*

## Practice Quiz: Assessing Your Knowledge

Below are some questions to help you review the content in the chapter. Answers to the questions are provided for you at the end of the Student Study Guide. Circle the correct answer for each question.

1. Which type of TBI results from the brain being whipped back and forth?
   PRAXIS 1            CEC 2
   A. Open head injury
   B. Closed head injury
   C. Anoxia
   D. Congenital brain injury

2. Which part of the brain is responsible for personality, emotions, problem solving, and reasoning?
   PRAXIS 1            CEC 2
   A. Brainstem
   B. Cerebellum
   C. Frontal lobe
   D. Temporal lobe

3. What category of changes includes seizures, increased spasticity, physical weakness, and fatigue?
   PRAXIS 1            CEC 2
   A. Physical changes
   B. Cognitive changes
   C. Linguistic changes
   D. Social, behavioral, and personality changes

4. What category of changes includes difficulty paying attention, difficulty problem solving, and forgetting facts or events?    PRAXIS 1            CEC 2
   A. Physical changes
   B. Cognitive changes
   C. Linguistic changes
   D. Social, emotional, and personality changes

5. What category of changes includes experiencing euphoria, restlessness, irritability, and anxiety?
   PRAXIS 1            CEC 2
   A. Physical changes
   B. Cognitive changes
   C. Linguistic changes
   D. Social, emotional, and personality changes

6. Which category of TBI causes tends to be mild and often goes unreported?   PRAXIS 1            CEC 2
   A. Child abuse
   B. Sports and recreational injuries
   C. Falls
   D. Auto accidents

7. Which medical exam identifies large areas of bleeding or large contusions?   PRAXIS 1            CEC 2
   A. CAT scan
   B. PET scan
   C. MRI
   D. WRAT-R

8. What is the usual reason why caretakers shake babies so violently that brain injury and sometimes death occur?
   PRAXIS 1                 CEC 2
   A. Because they are on drugs
   B. Because they were abused themselves
   C. Because they are drunk
   D. Because they want to stop the baby's crying

9. Which type of injury is most likely to be caused by a gunshot wound?          PRAXIS 1          CEC 2
   A. Open
   B. Closed
   C. Congenital
   D. Anoxia-related

10. Which of the following is not classified as TBI even though the brain is injured?          PRAXIS 1          CEC 2
    A. Tire iron blow to the head
    B. Bumping heads while on a trampoline
    C. Encephalitis
    D. Bicycle accidents

11. Rehabilitation helps to improve:          PRAXIS 3                 CEC 2
    A. Cognitive functioning
    B. Coordination and physical strength
    C. Independent functioning
    D. All of the above

12. Which group tends to have a greater impairment of cognitive abilities?          PRAXIS 1          CEC 2
    A. School-age children
    B. Infants and preschoolers
    C. Adolescents
    D. Adults

13. If the left hemisphere of the brain is damaged, which impairment is incurred?          PRAXIS 1          CEC 2
    A. Fine motor
    B. Communication
    C. Gross motor
    D. All are affected

14. What tends to be the most problematic and challenging area for students with TBI?  PRAXIS 1          CEC 2
    A. Motor control
    B. Communication
    C. Vision
    D. Behavior

15. Teachers need to use a checklist to evaluate the student with TBI:  PRAXIS 3                 CEC 5
    A. Every month
    B. Every 6 months
    C. Once a year for the IEP meeting
    D. Monthly the first year and then less frequently

Now that you have completed your chapter study, go back to the chapter objectives and see if you have truly met them. You may want to write out your responses to the chapter objectives so that you can check your understanding against the chapter outline or the text.

# Chapter 14: Understanding Students with Hearing Loss

## Objectives: Guiding Your Chapter Reading

The content in this chapter is presented to help you achieve the following objectives. Once you complete your study of the chapter, see if you can do what the objectives describe. If not, you may need to do some more reviewing of the chapter and your class notes.

- Define and identify the characteristics of students with hearing loss
- Recall the major causes of hearing loss
- Explain the assessment and evaluation practices for students with hearing loss
- Identify the major issues impacting students with hearing loss
- Describe successful instructional practices and accommodations for students with hearing loss

## Standards Matrices: Relating Content to Professional Standards

The matrices, or charts, below help you see how the professional standards from the Council for Exceptional Children (CEC) and PRAXIS™ apply to the content in this chapter. In addition, you can refer to the margin notes throughout the chapter and the activities at the end of each chapter to make sure you understand how these standards apply to the content in the field of special education. These standards are important for you to know because they provide the basis for the professional teacher certification examinations and content covered in these exams.

| CEC Standards | Chapter Topic |
|---|---|
| 1 | • IDEA <br> • Definition of hearing loss |
| 2 | • Case study <br> • Characteristics of hearing loss <br> • Causes of hearing loss |
| 3 | • Supplementary aids and services <br> • Universal design <br> • Testing accommodations |
| 4 | • Universal design <br> • Assistive technology <br> • Effective strategies as they relate to early childhood, middle school, and high school years <br> • Prelinguistic milieu teaching <br> • Shared reading <br> • The self-determined learning model of instruction <br> • Using authentic experiences <br> • Community-based instruction <br> • Cloze procedure |
| 5 | • Planning for other educational needs <br> • Using authentic experiences <br> • Inclusion |
| 6 | • Cochlear implants <br> • Assistive listening devices <br> • Communication methods <br> • A bilingual-bicultural model <br> • Prelinguistic milieu teaching |

| 7 | • Supplementary aids and services |
|---|---|
|   | • Using interpreters in educational settings |
|   | • Assistive technology |
|   | • Inclusion |
|   | • Appropriate education |
| 8 | • Evaluation and assessment |
|   | • Measuring student progress |
| 9 | • Characteristics of hearing loss |
|   | • Partnering for special education and related services |
| 10 | • Case study |
|   | • Partnering for special education and related services |
|   | • Planning for other educational needs |
|   | • Inclusion |

| PRAXIS™ Standards | Chapter Topic |
|---|---|
| 1 | • Case study |
|   | • Characteristics of hearing loss |
|   | • Causes of hearing loss |
| 2 | • IDEA |
|   | • Definitions of hearing loss |
| 3 | • Partnering for special education and related services |
|   | • Supplementary aids and services |
|   | • Universal design |
|   | • Testing accommodations |
|   | • Evaluation and assessment |
|   | • Measuring student progress |
|   | • Planning for other educational needs |
|   | • Inclusion |

## Checking for Understanding: Key Terms

To check that you understand the basic terms and vocabulary in the chapter, use the space provided to write the definitions or descriptions in your own words. Then, check the chapter to see how accurate your definition is, making sure you understand the context, or situation, in which the word is used. Reviewing these terms will help you better understand the concepts that support the content in this chapter.

| Term | Definition/Description | (✓) |
|---|---|---|
| unilateral hearing loss | | |
| bilateral hearing loss | | |
| hearing | | |

| Term | Definition/Description | (✓) |
|---|---|---|
| deaf | | |
| hard of hearing | | |
| congenital deafness | | |
| audition | | |
| Hertz (Hz) | | |
| decibels (dB) | | |
| auricle | | |
| pinna | | |
| malleus | | |
| incus | | |
| stapes | | |
| ossicular chain | | |
| eustachian tube | | |

| Term | Definition/Description | (✓) |
|---|---|---|
| oval window | | |
| cochlea | | |
| tonotopically | | |
| vestibular mechanism | | |
| speech reader | | |
| auditory verbal format | | |
| oral-aural form | | |
| manual approach | | |
| sign language | | |
| finger spelling | | |
| American Sign Language (ASL) | | |
| Pidgin Signed English (PSE) | | |
| Seeing Essential English | | |

| Term | Definition/Description | (✓) |
|---|---|---|
| Signing Exact English (SEE2) | | |
| Conceptually Accurate Signed English (CASE) | | |
| cued speech | | |
| congenital | | |
| hypoxia | | |
| rubella | | |
| toxoplasmosis | | |
| cytomegalovirus (CMV) | | |
| jaundice | | |
| anemia | | |
| hyperbilirubenemia | | |
| intracranial hemorrhage | | |
| maternal Rh incompatibility | | |

| Term | Definition/Description | (✓) |
|---|---|---|
| RhoGAM | | |
| bacterial meningitis | | |
| acute otitis media | | |
| otologist | | |
| audiologist | | |
| cochlear implant | | |
| audiometer | | |
| audiogram | | |
| tympanography | | |
| audiometry | | |
| field amplification system | | |
| loop systems | | |
| closed caption technology | | |

| Term | Definition/Description | (✓) |
|---|---|---|
| interpreter | | |
| cloze procedure | | |

## Chapter Outline: Taking Chapter Notes

The following outline is taken from the PowerPoint slides or overheads that your professor uses in class for this chapter. In the slides, there are several embedded links to more information for this chapter. Please go to the Companion Website at http://www.prenhall.com/turnbull to access them easily.

If you take your Student Study Guide to class, you can use this outline for taking notes on the chapter or for review. It will also allow you to listen to lectures and participate in class discussions without having to copy down all the PowerPoint information.

The notes below are set up for recording information from the chapter in a particular way—an adapted Cornell method of taking notes. In this adapted Cornell method, you underline, or highlight, information presented to you. In addition to highlighting, you can write information or explanations on the left-hand side of the table. Soon after the class presentation or reading the chapter, rewrite the notes from the left-hand side in your own words, using key terms and phrases. To study for quizzes or exams, you can cover up the left-hand side and use the right-hand side of the table to cue yourself about the information.

You also may just jot notes on the right-hand side to help you. Since this outline reduces the chapter for you, it will be a useful study aid. The summary at the end of the chapter is another useful resource to use for review.

| Chapter 14<br>Understanding Students with Hearing Loss | NOTES |
|---|---|
| [Slide 14-1] Chapter 14 Objectives: At the end of this chapter you should be able to:<br>• Define and identify the characteristics of students with hearing loss<br>• Recall the major causes of hearing loss<br>• Explain the assessment and evaluation practices for students with hearing loss<br>• Identify the major issues impacting students with hearing loss<br>• Describe successful instructional practices and accommodations for students with hearing loss | |

| | |
|---|---|
| [Slide 14-2] Who Are Mariah, Ricquel, and Shylah Thomas?<br>• Three sisters, ages 9, 7, and 3<br>• All three are profoundly deaf, and they are sisters to Bradley, age 11, who has no hearing loss<br>• They attend schools outside their neighborhood because their parents felt they could get a more appropriate education at other schools.<br>• They spend part of the day with teachers of the deaf and part of the day in general education<br>• They all have cochlear implants, a controversial treatment<br>    ▪ Some people believe it alters a person's inherent deafness and may diminish their worth<br>    ▪ There is a strong Deaf culture that opposes cochlear implants<br>• Form of communication is one of the most crucial decisions parents of children with hearing impairments must make | |
| [Slide 14-3] Defining Hearing Loss<br>• Deaf and hard of hearing describe hearing loss<br>• Unilateral (loss in one ear) and bilateral (loss in both ears)<br>• IDEA defines deafness as a hearing impairment that is so severe that the student is impaired in processing linguistic information through hearing, with or without amplification, and that it adversely affects the student's educational performance<br>• The severity of hearing loss is measured through decibels (dB)<br>    ▪ Deaf = 70–90 dB<br>    ▪ Hard of hearing = 20–70 dB<br>• Congenital deafness is a rare condition<br>• The Deaf community prefers the term *deaf child* to *hearing impaired* | |
| [Slide 14-4] Prevalence of Hearing Loss<br>• Low incidence disability<br>• In 2002–2003, 70,349 students with hearing loss between the ages of 6 and 21 received some type of special education services (U.S. Dept. of Ed.)<br>• Preschool programs (ages 3 to 5) served another 7,474 children, equivalent to about 1% of the total numbers of young children in preschools | |
| [Slide 14-5] Degrees of Hearing Loss (See Figure 14–1) | |

| | |
|---|---|
| [Slide 14-6] The Hearing Process<br>• Hearing Process: Audition<br>• Sound waves are vibrations in the air<br>• Sound is measured in units that describe the frequency and intensity of these vibrations:<br>  ▪ Intensity: measured in decibels (dB)<br>  ▪ Frequency: measured in Hertz (Hz)<br>  ▪ Results are charted on audiograms | |
| [Slide 14-7] Anatomical Structures of the Ear (See Figure 14–3) | |
| [Slide 14-8] Characteristics<br>• Speech and English language development<br>  ▪ Delays in language development<br>  ▪ Communication options:<br>    • Oral/aural<br>    • Manual communication<br>    • Sign language and finger spelling<br>    • American Sign Language (ASL)<br>    • Manually coded English<br>• Total or simultaneous communication | |
| [Slide 14-9] Academic Achievement<br>• Because educational curricula are so language-based, communication and learning are strongly linked<br>• There are rising numbers of students with hearing loss from diverse backgrounds<br>• Students who are hard of hearing are among the least appropriately served group | |
| [Slide 14-10] Social and Emotional Development<br>• Communication barriers affect a student's social and emotional development<br>• Four factors affect this development:<br>  ▪ parent-child interaction<br>  ▪ peers and teachers<br>  ▪ awareness of social cues<br>  ▪ an increasing sense of isolation and loneliness | |

| | |
|---|---|
| [Slide 14-11] Determining the Causes<br>• Congenital—present at birth<br>• Acquired—developed after birth<br>• Genetic causes<br>• Prenatal causes<br>    ▪ Hypoxia (lack of oxygen)<br>    ▪ Rubella<br>    ▪ Other illnesses, such as toxoplasmosis, herpes virus, syphilis, and cytomegalovirus (CMV)<br>    ▪ Premature infants<br>• Postnatal causes<br>    ▪ Bacterial meningitis<br>    ▪ Acute otitis media (ear infection)<br>• Postlingual causes<br>    ▪ Trauma to skull, excessive noise | |
| [Slide 14-12] Nondiscriminatory Evaluation Process (See Figure 14–6) | |
| [Slide 14-13] Determining the Presence<br>• Diagnostic Assessment<br>    ▪ Screen all newborns for hearing loss before 1 month of age<br>    ▪ Evaluate all infants who screen positive before 3 months<br>    ▪ Early intervention begun before 6 months<br>• Medical personnel<br>    ▪ Otologist (physician)<br>    ▪ Audiologist (measures hearing)<br>• Hearing aids<br>• Cochlear implants<br>• Assistive listening devices | |
| [Slide 14-14] Determining the Nature of Specially Designed Instruction and Services<br>• Educational evaluation<br>• How hearing is tested<br>    ▪ Audiometer<br>    ▪ Audiogram (behavioral)<br>    ▪ Tympanography<br>    ▪ Speech audiometry<br>• Stanford Achievement Test, tenth edition | |

| | |
|---|---|
| [Slide 14-15] Designing an Appropriate IEP<br>• Partnering for Special Education and Related Services<br>    ▪ Using interpreters in educational settings<br>• Determining Supplementary Aids and Services<br>    ▪ Managing the listening environment (acoustics)<br>• Hearing Aid: Loop Systems<br>    ▪ Assistive technology<br>• Closed Captioned Technology<br>    ▪ Computers and the Internet<br>    ▪ C-print : Real-time speech translations | |
| [Slide 14-16] Designing an Appropriate IEP<br>• Planning for Universal Design for Learning<br>    ▪ Communication methods<br>    ▪ Total communication fallen out of favor<br>    ▪ Debates over manual coded English<br>    ▪ Bilingual/bicultural model<br>• Planning for Other Educational Needs<br>    ▪ Few residential schools<br>    ▪ Must make an effort to preserve Deaf culture | |
| [Slide 14-17] Early Childhood Students<br>• Language-Rich Environments<br>• Early intervention<br>    ▪ Reggio Emilia<br>• Shared reading | |
| [Slide 14-18] Elementary and Middle School Students<br>• Reading and Writing Intervention<br>    ▪ Use authentic experiences<br>    ▪ Integrate vocabulary development<br>    ▪ Create opportunities for self-expression<br>    ▪ Provide deaf role models<br>    ▪ Teach about deaf studies | |
| [Slide 14-19] Secondary and Transition Students<br>• Community-based instruction<br>• Transition planning<br>    ▪ Students' interests and understanding<br>    ▪ Parents' insights into student and opportunities<br>    ▪ Assess student's communication and social skills<br>    ▪ Examine necessary accommodations<br>    ▪ Determine entry-level examination issues<br>    ▪ Explore financial needs and opportunities for postsecondary education<br>    ▪ Investigate workplace availability<br>• Postsecondary education | |
| [Slide 14-20] Educational Placement (See Figure 14–8) | |

| | |
|---|---|
| [Slide 14-21] Measuring Students' Progress<br>• Problems assessing students with hearing loss<br>• Reading and Writing Assessments<br>    ▪ Cloze procedure<br>    ▪ Oral reading test<br>    ▪ Story retelling<br>    ▪ Writing assessment | |
| [Slide 14-22] Measuring Students' Progress<br>• Progress in addressing other educational needs<br>    ▪ Collaboration needed between itinerant deaf teacher and direct services teacher<br>    ▪ Portfolio assessment<br>• Making accommodations for assessment<br>    ▪ Assistance before test on new forms of testing<br>    ▪ Longer time period<br>    ▪ Interpreting the directions<br>    ▪ Changing the format and content (rephrasing) | |
| [Slide 14-23] Looking to Mariah's, Ricquel's, and Shylah's Future<br>• Sharon wants her children to be "as normal as possible"<br>• This goal conflicts with their loyalty to the Deaf culture<br>• Mariah may become a physical education teacher<br>• Ricquel may follow a career in computers<br>• Shylah may become a professor of special education, concentrating on deaf education | |

## Activities: Applying Your Learning

Just as the textbook described Universal Design for Learning as the way for you to teach children, the principles work well for adult learners too. Rather than just taking notes, taking quizzes, and writing essays, the following activities will help you to learn the material on a deeper level and remember it better.

1. Etiquette for Interacting with Students with Hearing Loss. Read the following excerpt. Much of it was already discussed in the textbook chapter.

***Etiquette for Interacting with People with Hearing Loss. Taken from UCP (United Cerebral Palsy) website*** http://www.ucp.org/ucp_channeldoc.cfm/1/13/12632/12632-12632/6187 (also accessed through the Companion Website at www.prenhall.com/turnbull).

- When communicating with a person with a hearing impairment, be sure you have his or her attention by touching him or her lightly on the shoulder or waving your hand.
- Look directly at the person and speak clearly and at a comfortable pace to establish if the person can read lips (not all people with hearing impairments can lip-read). Those who can will rely on facial expressions, other body language, and gestures to help in understanding, so speak expressively but do not exaggerate your lip movement or shout. (Note: It is estimated that only 4 out of 10 spoken words are visible on the lips.) Show your consideration by placing yourself facing the light source and keeping your hands, cigarettes, and food away from your mouth when speaking. Brief, concise written notes may be helpful.
- In the United States, most people who are deaf use American Sign Language (ASL). ASL is not, however, a universal language. It is a language with its own syntax and grammatical structure. When scheduling an interpreter for a non-English-speaking person, be certain to retain an interpreter that speaks and interprets in the language of the person with the hearing impairment.
- Interpreters facilitate communication. They should not be consulted about matters concerning the person for whom they are interpreting.
- Do not shout at a person with a hearing impairment. Shouting distorts sounds accepted through hearing aids and inhibits lip reading.
- In order to facilitate conversation, be prepared to offer visual cues to a person with a hearing impairment when appropriate, especially when more than one person is speaking.

Which of the above etiquette statements have you "violated "in the past?

Which of the above etiquette statements will be the most difficult to follow in the future?

Are there any suggestions you disagree with? Why or why not?

2. Do you know anything about Deaf history? View the timeline at http://www.pbs.org/wnet/soundandfury/culture/deafhistory.html (also found at the Companion Website at www.prenhall.com/turnbull).

Which items were you familiar with?

Which items were you unfamiliar with?

Why is it important to understand the history of one's culture?

3. Other interactive activities are available at the Companion Website found at http://www.prenhall.com/turnbull. The site has several video clips and interactive activities called "Sound and Fury" to explore the controversy over cochlear implants and the Deaf community. There are also finger spelling activities and a free hearing screening. Make sure to read the personal stories and case studies about individuals with hearing loss.

4. Do not forget the DVD cases packaged with your textbook. There you can see video clips of the individuals discussed in the book.

Use your *Real Lives & Exceptionalities* DVD to see Star doing American Sign Language. Click on "Who is Star" (Clip 1) under "Meet Star." Why is sign language useful to students even if they do not have a hearing loss?

Use your *Real Lives & Exceptionalities* DVD to meet George, who has hearing loss. Click on "Meet George" and, while watching the clips, look for specific communication barriers he faces. How does George, his family, his teachers, and his peers foster his development?

*The questions that correspond to the DVD case studies are on the DVD, but they are also found in the back of this Student Study Guide. This will allow you to see the questions ahead of time. You are also welcome to write notes or answer the questions before typing them on the DVD.*

## Practice Quiz: Assessing Your Knowledge

Below are some questions to help you review the content in the chapter. Answers to the questions are provided for you at the end of the Student Study Guide. Circle the correct answer for each question.

1.  Which term refers to the number of vibrations that occur in one second?     PRAXIS 3          CEC 8
    A.  Loudness
    B.  Decibel
    C.  Intensity
    D.  Frequency

2.  The Deaf community prefer that their children be called:   PRAXIS 1          CEC 2
    A.  Hearing impaired child
    B.  Deaf child
    C.  Child with deafness
    D.  Child with a hearing impairment

3.  What (two) different aspects of assessed hearing are revealed on an audiogram?     PRAXIS 3          CEC 8
    A.  Pitch and loudness
    B.  Pitch and Hertz
    C.  Loudness and decibels
    D.  Intensity and pressure

4.  Why is learning language the single greatest challenge for children who are hard of hearing?
          PRAXIS 3          CEC2
    A.  Because there are three different forms of language used by individuals who are deaf or hard of hearing
    B.  Because the auditory information they receive is incomplete or distorted
    C.  Because teachers are not generally well prepared to teach language skills
    D.  Because the form of language taught in the schools may not match the form used in the home or in the Deaf community

5.  Which form of communication is Jeri using when she uses the manual alphabet to spell words letter by letter?
          PRAXIS 3          CEC 3
    A.  Oral/aural
    B.  Finger spelling
    C.  Simultaneous communication
    D.  Manual coded English

6.  The child with a hearing impairment also has an impairment in:     PRAXIS 1          CEC 2
    A.  Motor skills
    B.  Finger spelling
    C.  Language
    D.  Vision

7.  Which common virus remains inactive in the body but can be contracted by the fetus or the infant through breast milk? PRAXIS 1          CEC 2
    A.  Cytomegalovirus
    B.  Otitis media
    C.  Rubella
    D.  Meningitis

8.  Which type of hearing loss describes John, whose loss was caused by a syndrome that was present at birth?
          PRAXIS 1          CEC 2
    A.  Conductive
    B.  Postlingual
    C.  Sensorineural
    D.  A and C

9.  Decibels describe which part of the hearing assessment?   PRAXIS 3          CEC 8
    A.  Loudness
    B.  Pitch
    C.  Intensity
    D.  Pressure

10. How many different sounds are there in the English language?   PRAXIS 3          CEC 8
    A.  30
    B.  44
    C.  100
    D.  26

11. Which system/device requires that the teacher (or fellow classmates) wear a wireless microphone while the child who is deaf or hard of hearing wears the receiver?   PRAXIS 3          CEC 5
    A.  Hearing aid
    B.  Cochlear implant
    C.  FM system
    D.  Speech processor

12. Which of the following are strongly linked to the educational curricula?   PRAXIS 3          CEC 3
    A.  Learning and vision
    B.  Learning and communication
    C.  Learning and educational achievement
    D.  Learning and hearing

13. Which of the following was a result of the Americans with Disabilities Act?   PRAXIS 2          CEC 1
    A.  Individuals who are deaf or hard of hearing were guaranteed a free, appropriate education
    B.  Children who are deaf or hard of hearing could be educated in the public schools
    C.  Individuals who are deaf or hard of hearing had greater access to technologies such as TDDs
    D.  Individuals who are deaf or hard of hearing were guaranteed jobs in their chosen field

14. Which type of hearing test involves placing sensors on the baby's head and in the ear to monitor the baby's response to computer clicks?   PRAXIS 3          CEC 8
    A.  Behavioral audiological evaluation
    B.  Otoacoustic immittance test
    C.  Auditory brain stem test
    D.  Eustachian tube evaluation

15. Which device amplifies all sound and is battery powered?   PRAXIS 3          CEC 8
    A.  Hearing aid
    B.  Cochlear implant
    C.  FM receiver
    D.  Telephone amplifier

Now that you have completed your chapter study, go back to the chapter objectives and see if you have truly met them. You may want to write out your responses to the chapter objectives so that you can check your understanding against the chapter outline or the text.

# Chapter 15: Understanding Students with Visual Impairments

## Objectives: Guiding Your Chapter Reading

The content in this chapter is presented to help you achieve the following objectives. Once you complete your study of the chapter, see if you can do what the objectives describe. If not, you may need to do some more reviewing of the chapter and your class notes.

- Define and identify the characteristics of students with visual impairments
- Recall the major causes of visual impairments
- Explain the assessment and evaluation practices for students with visual impairments
- Identify the major issues impacting students with visual impairments
- Describe successful instructional practices and accommodations for students with visual impairments

## Standards Matrices: Relating Content to Professional Standards

The matrices, or charts, below help you see how the professional standards from the Council for Exceptional Children (CEC) and PRAXIS™ apply to the content in this chapter. In addition, you can refer to the margin notes throughout the chapter and the activities at the end of each chapter to make sure you understand how these standards apply to the content in the field of special education. These standards are important for you to know because they provide the basis for the professional teacher certification examinations and content covered in these exams.

| CEC Standards | Chapter Topic |
|---|---|
| 1 | • IDEA<br>• Definition of visual impairment |
| 2 | • Case study<br>• Characteristics of visual impairments<br>• Causes of visual impairment<br>• Limitations in the ability to get around<br>• Limitations in interactions with the environment |
| 3 | • Incidental learning<br>• Limitations in range and variety of experiences<br>• Supplementary aids and services<br>• Braille<br>• Provision of adapted materials<br>• Universal design<br>• Testing accommodations |
| 4 | • Universal design<br>• Braille<br>• Effective strategies as they relate to early childhood, middle school, and high school years<br>• Programming that focuses on real experiences<br>• Accommodations to develop basic skills |
| 5 | • Planning for other educational needs<br>• Expanded core curriculum<br>• Self-advocacy<br>• Inclusion |
| 6 | |
| 7 | • Supplementary aids and services<br>• Braille<br>• Inclusion<br>• Learning contracts |

| 8 | • Evaluation and assessment |
| | • Measuring student progress |
| | • Product evaluation |
| 9 | • Characteristics of visual impairment |
| | • Partnering for special education and related services |
| 10 | • Case study |
| | • Partnering for special education and related services |
| | • Planning for other educational needs |
| | • Inclusion |
| | • Transition |

| PRAXIS™ Standards | Chapter Topic |
|---|---|
| 1 | • Case study |
| | • Characteristics of visual impairments |
| | • Causes of visual impairment |
| 2 | • IDEA |
| | • Definitions of visual impairment |
| 3 | • Partnering for special education and related services |
| | • Supplementary aids and services |
| | • Universal design |
| | • Testing accommodations |
| | • Evaluation and assessment |
| | • Measuring student progress |
| | • Planning for other educational needs |
| | • Inclusion |
| | • Programming that focuses on real experiences |
| | • Accommodations to develop basic skills |
| | • Transition |

## Checking for Understanding: Key Terms

To check that you understand the basic terms and vocabulary in the chapter, use the space provided to write the definitions or descriptions in your own words. Then, check the chapter to see how accurate your definition is, making sure you understand the context, or situation, in which the word is used. Reviewing these terms will help you better understand the concepts that support the content in this chapter.

| Term | Definition/Description | (✓) |
|---|---|---|
| legal blindness | | |
| acuity | | |
| field of vision | | |

| Term | Definition/Description | (✓) |
|---|---|---|
| tunnel vision | | |
| visual disability (including blindness) | | |
| low vision | | |
| functionally blind | | |
| totally blind | | |
| incidental learning | | |
| congenital blindness | | |
| adventitious | | |
| etiology | | |
| functional vision assessment | | |
| low vision specialist | | |
| learning medium | | |
| learning medium assessment | | |

| Term | Definition/Description | (✓) |
|------|------------------------|-----|
| expanded core curriculum | | |
| orientation and mobility | | |
| slate and stylus | | |
| abacus | | |
| Braille | | |
| Braille contractions | | |

## Chapter Outline: Taking Chapter Notes

The following outline is taken from the PowerPoint slides or overheads that your professor uses in class for this chapter. In the slides, there are several embedded links to more information for this chapter. Please go to the Companion Website at http://www.prenhall.com/turnbull to access them easily.

If you take your Student Study Guide to class, you can use this outline for taking notes on the chapter or for review. It will also allow you to listen to lectures and participate in class discussions without having to copy down all the PowerPoint information.

The notes below are set up for recording information from the chapter in a particular way—an adapted Cornell method of taking notes. In this adapted Cornell method, you underline, or highlight, information presented to you. In addition to highlighting, you can write information or explanations on the left-hand side of the table. Soon after the class presentation or reading the chapter, rewrite the notes from the left-hand side in your own words, using key terms and phrases. To study for quizzes or exams, you can cover up the left-hand side and use the right-hand side of the table to cue yourself about the information.

You also may just jot notes on the right-hand side to help you. Since this outline reduces the chapter for you, it will be a useful study aid. The summary at the end of the chapter is another useful resource to use for review.

| Chapter 15<br>Understanding Students with Visual Impairments | NOTES |
|---|---|
| [Slide 15-1] Chapter 15 Objectives: At the end of this chapter you should be able to:<br>• Define and identify the characteristics of students with visual impairments<br>• Recall the major causes of visual impairments<br>• Explain the assessment and evaluation practices for students with visual impairments<br>• Identify the major issues impacting students with visual impairments<br>• Describe successful instructional practices and accommodations for students with visual impairments | |
| [Slide 15-2] Who Is Haley Sumner?<br>• She is a second grade student who has the ability to perceive light but is otherwise blind<br>• Haley began working with Miss Katie, a special educator, at the age of three and has become a very independent girl<br>• She can read Braille at the third grade level<br>• She can also read the Nemeth code, a special Braille code for math and science<br>• Miss Katie also teaches Haley orientation and mobility skills<br>• Haley views one of her biggest obstacles as people who don't believe she can do things on her own | |
| [Slide 15-3] Defining Visual Impairments<br>• Two different definitions<br>  ▪ Legal definition<br>    • Based on acuity and field of vision<br>  ▪ IDEA definition<br>    • Low vision<br>    • Functionally blind<br>    • Totally blind | |
| [Slide 15-4] Prevalence of Visual Impairments<br>• Various measures used, so it is difficult to get an accurate count<br>• Best estimates: 1–2 students in 1,000<br>• About 0.04 percent of the special education population | |

| | |
|---|---|
| [Slide 15-5] Characteristics<br>• Incidental learning<br>    ▪ The way sighted children naturally learn about their environment<br>    ▪ Lack of incidental learning skills can impact the development of motor, language, cognitive, and social skills<br>    ▪ Limitations in range and variety of experiences<br>    ▪ Limitations in the ability to get around<br>    ▪ Limitations in interactions with the environment | |
| [Slide 15-6] Determining the Causes<br>• Congenital vision impairments<br>    ▪ Occur at birth or before vision memories have been established<br>• Adventitious vision impairments<br>    ▪ When a person has had normal vision but then acquires a vision loss | |
| [Slide 15-7] Anatomy of the Eye (See Figure 15–2) | |
| [Slide 15-8] Nondiscriminatory Evaluation (See Figure 15–3) | |
| [Slide 15-9] Determining the Presence of Visual Impairment<br>• Determining how a student uses vision<br>    ▪ Functional vision assessment (FVA) provides more concrete information about a student's vision that may help in making IEP decisions<br>• Determining the appropriate reading medium<br>    ▪ Finding the appropriate learning medium (learning media assessment)<br>        • Braille, print, audiotapes, and access technology<br>    ▪ Allows the IEP team to know needed accommodations | |

| | |
|---|---|
| [Slide 15-10] Determining the Nature of Specially Designed Instruction and Services<br>• Expanded core curriculum<br>    ▪ Compensatory and communication skills<br>    ▪ Social and interaction skills<br>    ▪ Orientation and mobility skills<br>• Informal assessments should include the student's ability to function independently<br>• Assessments should include the age-appropriateness of tasks<br>    ▪ What are the student's peers doing?<br>    ▪ Determine skills typically learned through incidental learning, analyze task involvement, and begin teaching these tasks earlier<br>• Avoid making assumptions about a student's previously acquired learning | |
| [Slide 15-11] Partnering for Special Education and Related Services<br>• Nearly 69% spend most of their day in the general education classroom<br>• In planning an IEP, team members must consider:<br>    ▪ Provision of instruction to support the child's success in the general education curriculum<br>    ▪ Non-academic priorities on which the special education team will focus<br>    ▪ Location of special education and related services<br>    ▪ Ways in which they will communicate to meet the student's needs | |
| [Slide 15-12] Partnering for Special Education and Related Services<br>• Providing specialized instruction<br>    ▪ Slate and stylus<br>    ▪ Abacus<br>• Reading instruction<br>    ▪ Braille<br>    ▪ Braille contractions<br>    ▪ Issues for second language learners<br>• Determination of non-academic priorities<br>• Determining the location of services<br>• Communicating to meet student's needs | |

| | |
|---|---|
| [Slide 15-13] Developing an Appropriate IEP<br>• Determining Supplementary Aids and Services<br>    ▪ Providing adapted materials<br>        • Print materials: American<br>          Printing House for the Blind<br>        • Authentic materials<br>        • Optical devices<br>        • Assistive technology<br>• Planning for Universal Design for Learning<br>    ▪ NIMAS<br>    ▪ Direct experience and increased<br>      experiential activities | |
| [Slide 15-14] Planning for Other Educational Needs<br>• Daily living skills<br>• Orientation and mobility<br>• Self-advocacy<br>• Partnering is key | |
| [Slide 15-15] Early Childhood Students<br>• Programming That Focuses on Real Experiences<br>    ▪ BEGIN Foundation, Center for the<br>      Visually Impaired in Atlanta<br>    ▪ Benefits and involvement of parents<br>    ▪ Skills and strategies that are developed<br>    ▪ Emphasis on activities that are hands-on,<br>      meaningful, and related to real life | |
| [Slide 15-16] Elementary and Middle School<br>Students<br>• Accommodations to Develop Basic Skills<br>    ▪ Use Braille sheet music, tactile graphics<br>      such as maps with raised continents and<br>      tactilely different countries<br>    ▪ Describe specimens in science classes<br>    ▪ Teach students social skills so they can<br>      successfully be included | |
| [Slide 15-17] Secondary and Transition Students<br>• Preparing for Adult Life<br>    ▪ Secondary and transition programs focus<br>      on daily living skills<br>    ▪ Students work with O&M specialists<br>    ▪ Learn to navigate safely through new<br>      and unfamiliar environments<br>    ▪ Crucial to develop independent living<br>      skills | |
| [Slide 15-18] Educational Placement (See Figure<br>15–8) | |

| | |
|---|---|
| [Slide 15-19] Measuring Students' Progress<br>• Many students take the same math, social studies, language arts, and science tests as others<br>    ▪ Transcribe print materials into Braille<br>    ▪ Allow use of a magnifier when reading the test<br>    ▪ When students prepare Braille answers, the specialist interlines their work for the general educator (writes in print exactly what is written in Braille above the Braille)<br>    ▪ For Braille spelling tests, students spell the words both with and without the Braille contractions | |
| [Slide 15-20] Progress in Addressing Other Educational Needs<br>• Students' skill levels are determined through informal measures such as teacher observation, evaluation of needed prompt levels, and curriculum-based tests<br>• Teachers must have knowledge of the kinds of skill development influenced by the visual impairment and the related limitations in incidental learning | |
| [Slide 15-21] Making Accommodations for Assessments<br>• Additional time is needed<br>• Braille and/or magnifiers<br>• Reader<br>• Scribe or computer<br>• Quiet testing area<br>• Frequent breaks | |
| [Slide 15-22] Looking to Haley's Future<br>• Her future is bright because all partners in her education have kept high expectations since she was an infant<br>• They have looked ahead to see what skills she will need and designed educational programs to teach those skills<br>• Her team is making sure that Haley has all the tools she needs to be able to discover the world around her | |

## Activities: Applying Your Learning

Just as the textbook described Universal Design for Learning as the way for you to teach children, the principles work well for adult learners too. Rather than just taking notes, taking quizzes, and writing essays, the following activities will help you to learn the material on a deeper level and remember it better.

1. Retinal implants. Just as with cochlear implants there have been great technical advances in retinal implants. To see a simulation, go to "Artificial Alan" and click on the eye at http://www.pbs.org/saf/1209/features/artificialalan.htm (also found at our Companion Website at www.prenhall.com/turnbull). After completing the simulation, could you identify which woman's face you were seeing?

What kind of instructional accommodations would you still need to do for a student with a retinal implant?

2. Expanded Core Curriculum. Much of our learning is incidental and learned naturally through viewing others (social learning). Since students who are blind do not have incidental learning, they need an expanded curriculum to make sure they are able to function. Which of the following skills were you taught at home? At school? On your own? By peers?

| Expanded Core Curriculum (See Figure 15–3 in your textbook for details) | Where did you learn these skills? |
|---|---|
| Concept Development and Academic Skills | |
| Social/Emotional Skills | |
| Orientation and Mobility Skills | |
| Communication Skills | |
| Sensory/Motor Skills | |
| Daily Living Skills | |
| Career and Vocational Skills | |

Though not in the basic curriculum, how beneficial would it be if more of these skills were in the core curriculum for individuals without disabilities?

3. Other interactive activities are available at the Companion Website found at http://www.prenhall.com/turnbull. The STAR Legacy module helps you explore the challenges of teaching students with visual impairments. There are also several simulations of what it is like to have different vision problems. The American Federation of the Blind has a fun website to teach children about Braille and has an interesting overview of Helen Keller.

4. Do not forget the DVD cases packaged with your textbook. There you can see video clips of the individuals discussed in the book.

Use your *Real Lives & Exceptionalities* DVD to view Kristen, a woman with a visual impairment. Click on "Beyond School" and then select "Kristen" (Clip 7).   Kristen's mother says that she believes Kristen will always need "someone to trust" to help her with certain tasks. What kind of assistance might Haley (from your textbook) continue to require into adulthood?

Using your *Real Lives & Exceptionalities* DVD to view Kristen (Clip 7), located under "Beyond School," how would you work with Haley so that she is able to participate in the kinds of community-based activities accessed by Kristen?

*The questions that correspond to the DVD case studies are on the DVD, but they are also found in the back of this Student Study Guide. This will allow you to see the questions ahead of time. You are also welcome to write notes or answer the questions before typing them on the DVD.*

## Practice Quiz: Assessing Your Knowledge

Below are some questions to help you review the content in the chapter. Answers to the questions are provided for you at the end of the Student Study Guide. Circle the correct answer for each question.

1. Which person below has tunnel vision?    PRAXIS 1    CEC 2
   A. Audrey, whose visual acuity is 20/60 and field of vision is 140 degrees.
   B. Bertha, whose visual acuity is 20/40 and field of vision is 15 degrees.
   C. Cassie, whose visual acuity is 20/200 and field of vision is 25 degrees.
   D. None of the above

2. Which condition below refers to an individual who typically uses Braille for reading and writing, relies on his or her vision for other tasks, and uses his or her vision as well as tactile and auditory means for learning?    PRAXIS 1    CEC 2
   A. Low vision
   B. Functionally blind
   C. Totally blind
   D. Mixed blind

3. Although all of these areas present challenges, which of the following is especially problematic for all children with vision impairments?    PRAXIS 1    CEC 2
   A. Daily living skills
   B. Career and vocational skills
   C. Communication skills
   D. Incidental learning

4. Which of the following would have been reported to the teacher as a result of a functional vision evaluation?    PRAXIS 3    CEC 8
   A. "Misty has 20/120 vision."
   B. "Gretchen can identify classmates at 30 feet."
   C. "Matty's reading level is early second grade."
   D. "Michael can navigate the school surrounding with 90% accuracy using his cane."

5. Which of the following statements would be a conclusion from a learning media assessment?    PRAXIS 1    CEC 8
   A. "Braille is the most appropriate vehicle for teaching Lisa reading."
   B. "Suzanne enjoys all media—including listening to tapes, old records, and 'watching' TV."
   C. "Mae's intellectual skills are at the 50th percentile."
   D. Edwardo's IEP goal areas should be in daily living skills and mobility."

6. Which broad area includes skills such as using the telephone book, shopping, and preparing food?    PRAXIS 3    CEC 4
   A. Career and vocational skills
   B. Communication skills
   C. Social/emotional skills
   D. Daily living skills

7. Which broad area includes skills such as developing directional concepts, developing spatial concepts, and understanding traffic and traffic control?    PRAXIS 3    CEC 4
   A. Concept development and academic skills
   B. Orientation and mobility skills
   C. Daily living skills
   D. Sensory/motor skills

8. Which type of assessments are typically timed?   PRAXIS 3          CEC 8
   A. Norm-referenced tests
   B. Family interviews
   C. Checklists
   D. Authentic assessments

9. What is the "dark side" of technology for students with visual impairments?   PRAXIS 3      CEC 7
   A. The rising costs of technology make their use difficult to fund
   B. The rapid changes in technology make it difficult to for schools to keep up with the latest improvements
   C. Graphics-based sources make the general education curriculum less accessible
   D. Students outgrow their technologies at a rapid rate, thereby requiring more updates

10. Generally speaking, individuals below what age usually do not use a guide dog?   PRAXIS 1      CEC 2
    A. Age 15
    B. Age 18
    C. Age 21
    D. Age 28

11. Which specialist determines if a visual disorder can be corrected through lenses or optical devices?
    PRAXIS 3          CEC 8
    A. Orientation and mobility specialist
    B. Ophthalmologist
    C. Optometrist
    D. Audiologist

12. Which type of assistive technology scans printed material and creates a computer text file?
    PRAXIS 3          CEC 7
    A. Braille embossers
    B. Screen readers
    C. Optical character readers
    D. Screen navigation systems

13. What is the name for the shortcuts used to write common words or letter combinations in Braille?
    PRAXIS 3          CEC 7
    A. Braille notes
    B. Braille condensers
    C. Braille abbreviations
    D. Braille contractions

14. Which list below includes visual supports?   PRAXIS 3          CEC 7
    A. Graphic organizers, photographs, line drawings, sign language
    B. Cameras, telescopes, microscopes
    C. Glasses, large print books, cameras
    D. Assistive technology, magnifiers, large print books

15. Students with visual impairments need which of the following approaches for meaningful learning to take
    place?   PRAXIS 3          CEC 4
    A. Direct instruction approach
    B. Indirect instruction approach
    C. Hands-on approach
    D. Computer approach

Now that you have completed your chapter study, go back to the chapter objectives and see if you have truly met them. You may want to write out your responses to the chapter objectives so that you can check your understanding against the chapter outline or the text.

# Chapter 16: Understanding Students Who Are Gifted and Talented

## Objectives: Guiding Your Chapter Reading

The content in this chapter is presented to help you achieve the following objectives. Once you complete your study of the chapter, see if you can do what the objectives describe. If not, you may need to do some more reviewing of the chapter and your class notes.

- Define and identify the characteristics of students identified as gifted and talented
- Recall the major causal factors associated with students identified as gifted and talented
- Explain the assessment and evaluation practices for students identified as gifted and talented
- Identify the major issues impacting students identified as gifted and talented
- Describe successful instructional practices and accommodations for students identified as gifted and talented

## Standards Matrices: Relating Content to Professional Standards

The matrices, or charts, below help you see how the professional standards from the Council for Exceptional Children (CEC) and PRAXIS™ apply to the content in this chapter. In addition, you can refer to the margin notes throughout the chapter and the activities at the end of each chapter to make sure you understand how these standards apply to the content in the field of special education. These standards are important for you to know because they provide the basis for the professional teacher certification examinations and content covered in these exams.

| CEC Standards | Chapter Topic |
|---|---|
| 1 | • IDEA<br>• Definition of gifted and talented |
| 2 | • Case study<br>• Characteristics of gifted and talented<br>• Behavioral characteristics<br>• Social and emotional characteristics<br>• Determining the origins |
| 3 | • Gardner's multidimensional intelligences<br>• Creative productive thinking<br>• Leadership ability<br>• Visual and performing arts<br>• Supplementary aids and services<br>• Universal design<br>• Differentiated instruction<br>• Testing accommodations |
| 4 | • Universal design<br>• Effective strategies as they relate to early childhood, middle school, and high school years<br>• Project spectrum<br>  • School-wide enrichment program<br>  • Promoting creativity and critical thinking skills<br>  • Autonomous learning model |
| 5 | • Planning for other educational needs |
| 6 | |
| 7 | • Supplementary aids and services<br>• Inclusion<br>• Bloom's taxonomy<br>• Autonomous learning model |

| 8 | • Evaluation and assessment<br>• DISCOVER<br>• Measuring student progress<br>• Product evaluation<br>• Process evaluation |
|---|---|
| 9 | • Characteristics of gifted and talented<br>• Partnering for special education and related services |
| 10 | • Case study<br>• Partnering for special education and related services<br>• Planning for other educational needs<br>• Co-teaching<br>• Inclusion |

| PRAXIS™ Standards | Chapter Topic |
|---|---|
| 1 | • Case study<br>• Characteristics<br>• Determining the origins |
| 2 | |
| 3 | • Partnering for special education and related services<br>• Supplementary aids and services<br>• Universal design<br>• Testing accommodations<br>• Evaluation and assessment<br>• Measuring student progress<br>• Planning for other educational needs<br>• Inclusion<br>• Transition |

## Checking for Understanding: Key Terms

To check that you understand the basic terms and vocabulary in the chapter, use the space provided to write the definitions or descriptions in your own words. Then, check the chapter to see how accurate your definition is, making sure you understand the context, or situation, in which the word is used. Reviewing these terms will help you better understand the concepts that support the content in this chapter.

| Term | Definition/Description | (✓) |
|---|---|---|
| multidimensional model of intelligence | | |
| prodigy | | |
| differentiated instruction | | |

| | | |
|---|---|---|
| acceleration | | |
| compact the curriculum | | |
| curriculum extension | | |
| cognitive taxonomies | | |
| autonomous learning model | | |
| schoolwide enrichment model | | |
| cluster grouping | | |
| all-school enrichment programs | | |

## Chapter Outline: Taking Chapter Notes

The following outline is taken from the PowerPoint slides or overheads that your professor uses in class for this chapter. In the slides, there are several embedded links to more information for this chapter. Please go to the Companion Website at http://www.prenhall.com/turnbull to access them easily.

If you take your Student Study Guide to class, you can use this outline for taking notes on the chapter or for review. It will also allow you to listen to lectures and participate in class discussions without having to copy down all the PowerPoint information.

The notes below are set up for recording information from the chapter in a particular way—an adapted Cornell method of taking notes. In this adapted Cornell method, you underline, or highlight, information presented to you. In addition to highlighting, you can write information or explanations on the left-hand side of the table. Soon after the class presentation or reading the chapter, rewrite the notes from the left-hand side in your own words, using key terms and phrases. To study for quizzes or exams, you can cover up the left-hand side and use the right-hand side of the table to cue yourself about the information.

You also may just jot notes on the right-hand side to help you. Since this outline reduces the chapter for you, it will be a useful study aid. The summary at the end of the chapter is another useful resource to use for review.

| Chapter 16<br>**Understanding Students Who Are Gifted and Talented** | NOTES |
|---|---|
| [Slide 16-1] Chapter 16 Objectives: At the end of this chapter you should be able to:<br>• Define and identify the characteristics of students identified as gifted and talented<br>• Recall the major causal factors associated with students identified as gifted and talented<br>• Explain the assessment and evaluation practices for students identified as gifted and talented<br>• Identify the major issues impacting students identified as gifted and talented<br>• Describe successful instructional practices and accommodations for students identified as gifted and talented | |
| [Slide 16-2] Who is Briana Hoskins?<br>• Briana is a 16-year-old girl.<br>• She began showing signs of unique talent at the age of 3.<br>• She is enrolled in a school an hour away so she can receive appropriate services for her gifts.<br>• She tends to be shy and doesn't like people to know that she is gifted.<br>• Finding an education that challenges her appropriately has been difficult.<br>• She may skip the eighth grade and transition directly into high school; her mother and teachers are currently considering the possible social consequences. | |
| [Slide 16-3] Defining Giftedness<br>• Currently, 29 states have laws requiring schools to provide gifted and talented education; 19 states do not<br>• Most states define giftedness based on the Javits Gifted and Talented Act<br>• IDEA does not require states to provide services<br>• Criteria varies:<br>   ▪ Choose IQ level<br>   ▪ Choose a percentage of top students<br>   ▪ Determine how many will receive services<br>• Underrepresentation of student from diverse backgrounds | |

| | |
|---|---|
| [Slide 16-4] Gardner's Multiple Intelligences (See Figure 16–1)<br>• Musical<br>• Bodily-kinesthetic<br>• Logical-mathematical<br>• Linguistic<br>• Spatial<br>• Interpersonal<br>• Intrapersonal<br>• Naturalist | |
| [Slide 16-5] Describing the Characteristics<br>• High general intellect<br>    ▪ prodigy<br>• Creative, productive thinking<br>• Leadership ability<br>• Visual and performing arts<br>• Behavioral, social, and emotional characteristics<br>• Origin: Interaction between nature/nurture | |
| [Slide 16-6] Nondiscriminatory Evaluation (See Figure 16–3) | |
| [Slide 16-7] Evaluating Students<br>• Challenges identifying students from diverse backgrounds<br>• Use multiple means of measurement<br>• Multiple intelligences<br>    ▪ DISCOVER<br>• Creativity assessments<br>    ▪ Torrance Test of Creative Thinking<br>    ▪ Thinking Creatively with Words<br>    ▪ Thinking Creatively with Pictures | |
| [Slide 16-8] Partnering for Special Education and Related Services<br>• Differentiated instruction<br>    ▪ Involves differentiation strategies such as:<br>        • Flexible grouping<br>        • Learning stations/centers<br>        • Compacted/expanded curriculum<br>        • Co-teaching<br>    ▪ Partnerships | |

| | |
|---|---|
| [Slide 16-9] Determining Supplementary Aids and Services<br>• Acceleration<br>    ▪ Student moves more rapidly through the curriculum<br>    ▪ May include skipping classes or grades<br>• Compact the Curriculum<br>    ▪ Assess parts of the curriculum already mastered<br>    ▪ Teacher only teaches curriculum not already mastered<br>    ▪ May start by doing most difficult task first | |
| [Slide 16-10] Planning Universally Designed Learning and Other Educational Needs<br>• Curriculum extension<br>    ▪ Expand the breadth and depth<br>• Cognitive taxonomies (Bloom)<br>    ▪ Move students up to more complex tasks<br>• Autonomous learning model<br>    ▪ Explore what it means to be gifted<br>    ▪ Explore what intelligence and creativity mean<br>    ▪ Explore aspects of their personal/social development<br>    ▪ Consider their strengths and limitations<br>    ▪ Teach organizational skills<br>    ▪ Engage in self-directed study about topics of interest<br>    ▪ Teach the importance of autonomous life-long learning | |
| [Slide 16-11] Early Childhood Students<br>• Multiple intelligences<br>    ▪ Gifted programs for young children are fairly rare<br>    ▪ Project SPECTRUM<br>    ▪ Montgomery Knolls Early Childhood Gifted Program<br>    ▪ Focuses on identifying and serving different types of giftedness | |
| [Slide 16-12] Elementary and Middle School Students<br>• School-wide enrichment model<br>    ▪ Blue Valley School District, Kansas<br>    ▪ Integrates features of enriching experiences and problem-based learning<br>    ▪ Uses the school-wide enrichment model and the autonomous learner model<br>    ▪ Teachers view themselves as learning facilitators<br>• WebQuests | |

| | |
|---|---|
| [Slide 16-13] Secondary and Transition Students<br>• Promoting Creativity and Critical-Thinking Skills<br>    ▪ DISCOVER<br>        • Competitions:<br>            ▪ Math Counts<br>            ▪ Odyssey of the Mind<br>            ▪ Science Olympiad | |
| [Slide 16-14] Service Options<br>• Cluster grouping<br>• All-school enrichment programs<br>• Accelerative method<br>• Magnet schools, charter schools, self-contained classes, special day schools, residential schools | |
| [Slide 16-15] Measuring Student Progress<br>• Progress in the general curriculum<br>    ▪ Some evaluation responsibility on the student<br>• Product evaluation<br>• Process evaluation<br>    ▪ Reflective assessments<br>• Progress in addressing other educational needs<br>    ▪ Learning contracts | |
| [Slide 16-16] Making Accommodations for Assessments<br>• Usually do not need accommodation unless they also have a disability<br>• May feel added pressure to perform well<br>• SAT and ACT may exert extreme pressure, especially if students are competing for scholarships<br>• Test-taking techniques to help lower test anxiety | |
| [Slide 16-17] Looking to Briana's Future<br>• Briana may skip one grade and begin high school a year early.<br>• She will continue to strengthen her academic, artistic, and athletic skills.<br>• She is receiving offers from universities, summer sports camps, private conservatories, and dance troupes that would like her to join their institutions.<br>• She will need flexibility in her academic and extracurricular activities, acceleration in all her activities, and variety in the ways in which she learns and participates.<br>• She will need to determine how to maintain social acceptance and remain balanced emotionally. | |

## Activities: Applying Your Learning

Just as the textbook described Universal Design for Learning as the way for you to teach children, the principles work well for adult learners too. Rather than just taking notes, taking quizzes, and writing essays, the following activities will help you to learn the material on a deeper level and remember it better.

1. Multiple Intelligences. It is quite clear that there are many more intelligences than the two measured by traditional IQ tests. The textbook lists famous people that have those characteristics. But giftedness can be found closer to home. Rather than just looking at famous people, name a person you know who is gifted in each of the areas of intelligence.

| Type of Intelligence | Person You Know |
|---|---|
| Musical | |
| Bodily-kinesthetic | |
| Logical-mathematical | |
| Linguistic | |
| Spatial | |
| Interpersonal | |
| Intrapersonal | |
| Naturalist | |

Which intelligences do you possess?

2. Acceleration Versus Enrichment. The textbook discusses different strategies to teach students who are gifted or talented. Compare and contrast acceleration and enrichment. How are they similar? How are they different? What are the pros and cons of these two major approaches?

| Acceleration | Enrichment |
|---|---|
| | |

3. Other interactive activities are available at the Companion Website found at http://www.prenhall.com/turnbull. There is an interesting video that discusses the impact of NCLB on gifted programs. Also, there are case studies and interactive activities to explore what it means to be gifted and talented.

4. Do not forget the DVD cases packaged with your textbook. There you can see video clips of the individuals discussed in the book.

Use your *Real Lives & Exceptionalities* DVD to critically think about working with Briana under "Questions," located below "Meet Briana." Do you believe students who are gifted and talented should be required to have IEPs? How about federal funding allocated for special education? Why or why not?

*The questions that correspond to the DVD case studies are on the DVD, but they are also found in the back of this Student Study Guide. This will allow you to see the questions ahead of time. You are also welcome to write notes or answer the questions before typing them on the DVD.*

## Practice Quiz: Assessing Your Knowledge

Below are some questions to help you review the content in the chapter. Answers to the questions are provided for you at the end of the Student Study Guide. Circle the correct answer for each question.

1. Which one of the following qualities is not mentioned in the federal definition of gifted?
   PRAXIS 2          CEC 1
   A. Intellectual capability
   B. Artistic ability
   C. Intrapersonal skills
   D. Academic aptitude

2. Which one of the areas of intelligence is being illustrated by Johann, who has an intuitive sense of layout, is able to see many architectural perspectives when designing his own dream home, and notices fine details?
   PRAXIS 1          CEC 2
   A. Bodily-kinesthetic
   B. Logical-mathematical
   C. Spatial
   D. Naturalist

3. What are some early signs of possible giftedness?          PRAXIS 1          CEC 2
   A. An advanced vocabulary
   B. A reluctance to take risks
   C. An interest in spiritual issues
   D. All of the above

4. What two other conditions have characteristics that overlap giftedness?          PRAXIS 1          CEC 2
   A. Emotionally disturbed and communication disorders
   B. Emotionally disturbed and learning disabled
   C. AD/HD and learning disabled
   D. AD/HD and emotionally disturbed

5. What percentage of the population is considered gifted when only using IQ scores?   PRAXIS 1          CEC 2
   A. The top 10–12%
   B. The top 8–9%
   C. The top 5–6%
   D. The top 2–3 %

6. For which student below would the DISCOVER assessment be most appropriate?   PRAXIS 3          CEC 8
   A. Mary, a 4th grade midwesterner from a white middle-class family who speaks French fluently
   B. Brad, a 9th grader from Denver who is of European descent and is the oldest in his family
   C. Maria, a 3rd grader from Laredo, Texas, who speaks Spanish as her native language
   D. Sheldon, a 7th grade African American student from inner-city Chicago

7. What is the name of the test that assesses two aspects of creativity?          PRAXIS 3          CEC 8
   A. The Torrance Tests of Creative Thinking
   B. The DISCOVER Test of Creative Thinking
   C. The Multi-level Test of Thinking and Creating
   D. The Gardner Assessment of Creative Thinking

8. Which characteristic does Goleman use to explain why some people are more successful in life than others—regardless of their intellectual level?   PRAXIS 3          CEC 3
   A. Expertise
   B. Domain-specific giftedness
   C. Emotional intelligence
   D. Self-determination

9. Which type of evaluation is Mrs. Marie representing when she looks primarily at test scores for recommending students for services?　　　PRAXIS 3　　　　CEC 8
    A. Process evaluation
    B. Portfolio evaluation
    C. Formative evaluation
    D. Product evaluation

10. How can teachers adjust instruction to meet the needs of students who are gifted?　　PRAXIS 3　　CEC 4
    A. Tailor the pace of instruction
    B. Relate instruction to student interests
    C. Adjust the depth and breadth of content coverage
    D. All of the above

11. Which of the following is the first step in identifying students who may be gifted?　　PRAXIS 3　　CEC 8
    A. Determine their least restrictive environment
    B. Write their IEP
    C. Determine if they are gifted
    D. Provide necessary special education services

12. Many children who are gifted are often misidentified as being:　　PRAXIS 1　　　　CEC 2
    A. ADHD
    B. Learning disabled
    C. Emotionally disturbed
    D. A and B

13. A differentiated instructional classroom requires:　　PRAXIS 3　　　　CEC10
    A. Parents and general education teachers to partner together
    B. General education teachers and special education teachers to partner together
    C. Special education teachers and parents to partner together
    D. None of the above

14. The IEP team needs to consider which of the following?　PRAXIS 3　　　CEC 3
    A. Goals that are aligned with the standards
    B. Goals that challenge the student
    C. Goals that are aligned with grade-level expectations
    D. Goals that are aligned with the NCLB

15. When Chris makes a rain hat from a trash bag, he has engaged in which of the levels on Bloom's Taxonomy?
    　　PRAXIS 3　　　　CEC 5
    A. Knowledge
    B. Evaluation
    C. Synthesis
    D. Application

Now that you have completed your chapter study, go back to the chapter objectives and see if you have truly met them. You may want to write out your responses to the chapter objectives so that you can check your understanding against the chapter outline or the text.

# DVD Questions

These questions appear on the DVD that came with your book. You may choose to answer the questions here, if your professor prefers, or on the DVD. The questions give you a good review of the content on the DVD and also help you review and apply the information in the book. Remember that these are real people who live with their disabilities every day of their lives. Their exceptionalities truly make them exceptional individuals.

### Ryan
**School Connections: Who is Ryan?**
1. In the perception of Ryan's teachers and therapists, who is he and why is it important for them to know him?

**School Connections: Who is Ryan?**
2. In what ways has your own understanding and insights into Ryan's personality and abilities changed and grown during this study?

**School Connections: Accommodations**
3. In what ways does the program provided for Ryan by his school-based and community-based support team exhibit the attributes of what the text authors call "universally designed instruction"?

**School Connections: Accommodations**
4. In what ways can you make a case for the proposition that Ryan's support program is highly aligned with IDEA standards and philosophy as well as Section 504?

**School Connections: Collaboration**
5. Assume that you are given a leadership role for Ryan's school-based and community-based support team. What patterns would you keep and what would you change and why?

**School Connections: Collaboration**
6. Point out some of the critical reasons and/or circumstances where Ryan's school-based and community-based care providers must collaborate to fully serve his needs.

**Family Support: Ryan's Family**

7. What are Ryan's parents' attitudes toward Ryan at this point in his progress?

**Family Support: Ryan's Family**

8. What are some of the critical family dynamics that build on and support Ryan's strengths and needs?

**Family Support: Ryan's Family**

9. What are some of the advantages and disadvantages stemming from the fact that Ryan's mother is available to drive him to and from school?

**Family Support: Sibling**

10. What roles do you see Nicole, Ryan's sibling, playing in his growth and development?

**Family Support: Collaboration**

11. If you had to walk in Ryan's parents' shoes for one week, who are the service providers and other individuals/institutions with whom you would need to communicate and collaborate to fully support Ryan?

**Family Support: Collaboration**

12. The initiative for teaming and communication seems to rest at times with the school or the community and at times with the home. Provide examples from Ryan's life of school-initiated communication and community-initiated and home-initiated teaming.

**Community & Contributions: Extracurricular**

13. A familiar challenge for Ryan's support team is making decisions about planning for the physical accessibility of all of the places Ryan may want to go. What are the critical issues that his team must confront while making these important decisions?

**Community & Contributions: Extracurricular**

14. What case can be made for expecting and anticipating that Ryan's peers will provide important supports for his ongoing growth and development in addition to the services provided by professionals and family?

**Community & Contributions: Self-Determination**

15. In what ways has Ryan enriched and contributed to the lives of all those he associates with, including school, family, and community circles?

**Community & Contributions: Self-Determination**

16. In what ways can you perceive building on Ryan's strengths, e.g., his social skills, to involve him with the larger school and neighborhood community?

**Community & Contributions: Self-Determination**

17. Why is it so important for the members of Ryan's support team to envision his future as probably including such things as driving vehicles and attending higher education?

**Community & Contributions: Self-Determination**

18. What are some key thoughts, attitudes, and actions you might emulate in your work with exceptional children based on advice from members of Ryan's support team?

<u>Star</u>
**School Connections: Who is Star?**
1. In the perception of Star's teachers, therapists, and school leaders, who is she and why is it important for them to know her?

**School Connections: Who is Star?**
2. In what ways has your own understanding and insights into Star's personality and abilities changed and grown during this study?

**School Connections: Accommodations**
3. In what ways does the program provided for Star by her school-based support team exhibit the attributes of what the text authors call "universally designed instruction"?

**School Connections: Accommodations**
4. In what ways can you make a case for the proposition that Star's support program is highly aligned with IDEA standards and philosophy?

**School Connections: Collaboration**
5. Assume that you were given a leadership role for Star's school-based support team. What patterns would you keep, what would you change, and why?

**School Connections: Collaboration**
6. Point out some of the critical reasons and/or circumstances where Star's school-based care providers must collaborate to more fully serve her needs.

**Family Support: Star's Family**

7. Trace the journey and evolution of Barbara Morgan's thinking about adopting and caring for exceptional children from the time when she was a fully employed professional to her current role as parent in a house full of adopted young people.

**Family Support: Star's Family**

8. What are some of the critical family dynamics that build on and specifically support Star's strengths and needs?

**Family Support: Collaboration**

9. If you had to walk in Barbara Morgan's shoes for a week, who are the service providers and other individuals/institutions with whom you would need to communicate and collaborate to fully support Star?

**Family Support: Collaboration**

10. The initiative for teaming and communication seems to rest at times with the school and at times with the home. Provide examples from Star's life of school-initiated communication and home-initiated teaming.

**Family Support: Siblings**

11. Barbara Morgan has legally adopted Star and considers her to be one of her children. Compare and contrast the impact on Star of this adoptive relationship versus being temporarily cared for in a group home for foster children.

**Family Support: Siblings**

12. In what ways is Star's growth promoted by living in a family with several siblings where they all must abide by family rules and routines?

**Community & Contributions: Collaboration**

13. A familiar challenge for Star's support team is making decisions about when to place her among peers versus in one-on-one settings. What are the critical issues that her team must confront while making these important decisions?

**Community & Contributions: Collaboration**

14. What case can be made for expecting and anticipating that Star's peers will provide important supports for her ongoing growth and development in addition to the services provided by professionals and family?

**Community & Contributions: Collaboration**

15. In what ways has Star enriched and contributed to the lives of all those she associates with, including school, family, and community circles?

**Community & Contributions: Collaboration**

16. In what ways can you perceive building on Star's strengths, e.g., her signing skills, to involve her with the larger school and neighborhood community?

**Community & Contributions: Vision & Advice**

17. Why is it so important for members of Star's support team to envision her future?

**Community & Contributions: Vision & Advice**

18. What are some key thoughts, attitudes, and actions you might emulate in your work with exceptional children based on advice from members of Star's support team?

## George

**School Connections: Who is George?**

1. In the perception of George's teacher and therapists, who is he and why is it important for them to know him?

**School Connections: Who is George?**

2. In what ways has your own understanding and insights into George's personality and abilities changed and grown during this study?

**School Connections: Accommodations**

3. In what ways does the program provided for George by his school-based and community-based support team exhibit the attributes of what the text authors call "universally designed instruction"?

**School Connections: Accommodations**

4. In what ways can you make a case for the proposition that George's support program is highly aligned with IDEA standards and philosophy?

**School Connections: Collaboration**

5. Assume that you were given a leadership role for George's school-based and community-based support team. What patterns would you keep, what would you change, and why?

**School Connections: Collaboration**

6. Point out some of the critical reasons and/or circumstances where George's school-based and community-based care providers must collaborate to more fully serve his needs.

**Family Support: George's Family**

7. Medical practitioners informed George's parents that he would probably be a "vegetable" when he was first born. In what ways did his parents respond that convince us they did not accept that medical prognosis?

**Family Support: George's Family**

8. What are some of the critical family dynamics that build on and specifically support George's strengths and needs?

**Family Support: Collaboration**

9. If you had to walk in Philip and Linda Wedge's shoes for a week, who are the service providers and other individuals/institutions with whom you would need to communicate and collaborate to fully support George?

**Family Support: Collaboration**

10. The initiative for teaming and communication seems to rest at times with the school and the community and at times with the home. Provide examples from George's life of school-initiated communication and community-initiated and home-initiated teaming.

**Family Support: George's Family**

11. What are some of the advantages and disadvantages for George and his family to have parents that are both university and high school educators by profession and professional training?

**Family Support: Sibling**

12. What roles do you see Roy, George's big brother, playing in his growth and development?

**Community & Contributions: Collaboration**

13. A familiar challenge for George's support team is making decisions about when to place him among peers versus in one-on-one settings. What are the critical issues that his team must confront while making these important decisions?

**Community & Contributions: Collaboration**

14. What case can be made for expecting and anticipating that George's peers will provide important supports for his ongoing growth and development in addition to the services provided by professionals and family?

**Community & Contributions: Extracurricular**

15. In what ways has George enriched and contributed to the lives of all those he associates with, including school, family, and community circles?

**Community & Contributions: Extracurricular**

16. In what ways can you perceive building on George's strengths, e.g., his social, physical, and reading/writing skills, to involve him with the larger school and neighborhood community?

**Community & Contributions: Vision & Advice**

17. Why is it so important for members of George's support team to envision his future as probably including such things as playing and winning at chess and attending higher education?

**Community & Contributions: Vision & Advice**

18. What are some key thoughts, attitudes, and actions you might emulate in your work with exceptional children based on advice from members of George's support team, including the emphatic pronouncement given by his mother, "Never give up on a kid"?

<u>Heather</u>
**School Connections: Who is Heather?**
1. In the perception of Heather's teachers, therapists, and school leaders, who is she and why is it important for them to know her?

**School Connections: Who is Heather?**
2. In what ways has your own understanding and insights into Heather's personality and abilities changed and grown during this study?

**School Connections: Accommodations**
3. In what ways does the program provided for Heather by her school-based support team exhibit the attributes of what the text authors call "universally designed instruction"?

**School Connections: Accommodations**
4. In what ways can you make a case for the proposition that Heather's support program is highly aligned with IDEA standards and philosophy?

**School Connections: Collaboration**
5. Assume that you were given a leadership role for Heather's school-based support team. What patterns would you keep, what would you change, and why?

**School Connections: Collaboration**
6. Point out some of the critical reasons and/or circumstances where Heather's school-based care providers must collaborate to more fully serve her needs.

**Family Support: Heather's Family**

7. Barbara Morgan, Heather's adopted mother, provides a fascinating account of how Heather's outlandish behavior drastically changed once it was certain she was to become a genuine member of the Morgan family. Provide a psychological explanation of Heather's dramatic shift in attitude and behavior.

**Family Support: Heather's Family**

8. What are some of the critical family dynamics that build on and specifically support Heather's strengths and needs?

**Family Support: Collaboration**

9. If you had to walk in Barbara Morgan's shoes for a week, who are the service providers and other individuals/institutions with whom you would need to communicate and collaborate to fully support Heather?

**Family Support: Collaboration**

10. The initiative for teaming and communication seems to rest at times with the school and at times with the home. Provide examples from Heather's life of school-initiated communication and home-initiated teaming.

**Family Support: Sibling**

11. Barbara Morgan has legally adopted Heather and considers her to be one of her children. Compare and contrast the impact on Heather of this adoptive relationship versus being temporarily cared for in a group home for foster children.

**Family Support: Sibling**

12. In what ways is Heather's growth promoted by living in a family with several siblings where they all must abide by family rules and routines?

**Community & Contributions: Collaboration**

13. A familiar challenge for Heather's support team is making decisions about when to place her among peers versus in one-on-one settings. What are the critical issues that her team must confront while making these important decisions?

**Community & Contributions: Collaboration**

14. What case can be made for expecting and anticipating that Heather's peers will provide important supports for her ongoing growth and development in addition to the services provided by professionals and family?

**Community & Contributions: Extracurricular**

15. In what ways has Heather enriched and contributed to the lives of all those she associates with, including school, family, and community circles?

**Community & Contributions: Extracurricular**

16. In what ways can you perceive building on Heather's strengths, e.g., her courage to run for a student body office, to involve her with the larger school and neighborhood community?

**Community & Contributions: Vision & Advice**

17. Why is it so important for members of Heather's support team to envision her future?

**Community & Contributions: Vision & Advice**

18. What are some key thoughts, attitudes, and actions you might emulate in your work with exceptional children based on advice from members of Heather's support team?

### Briana

**School Connections: Who is Briana?**

1. In the perception of Briana's teachers, therapists, and school leaders, who is she and why is it important for them to know her?

**School Connections: Who is Briana?**

2. In what ways has your own understanding and insights into Briana's personality and abilities changed and grown during this study?

**School Connections: Accommodations**

3. In what ways does the program provided for Briana by her middle school and high school support teams exhibit the attributes of what the text authors call "universally designed instruction"?

**School Connections: Accommodations**

4. In what ways can you make a case for the proposition that Briana's support program is highly aligned with IDEA standards and philosophy?

**School Connections: Collaboration**

5. Assume that you were given a leadership role for Briana's school-based support teams. What patterns would you keep, what would you change, and why?

**School Connections: Collaboration**

6. Point out some of the critical reasons and/or circumstances where Briana's school-based care providers must collaborate to more fully serve her needs.

**Family Support: Briana's Family**

7. Deborah Hoskins, Briana's mother, has been her daughter's advocate since early in primary school. What are some of the essential elements of an effective parent advocate as exhibited by Briana's mother?

**Family Support: Briana's Family**

8. What are some of the critical family dynamics that build on and specifically support Briana's strengths and needs?

**Family Support: Collaboration**

9. If you had to walk in Deborah Hoskin's shoes for a school calendar year, who are the service providers and other individuals/institutions with whom you would need to communicate and collaborate to fully support Briana?

**Family Support: Collaboration**

10. The initiative for teaming and communication seems to rest at times with the school and at times with the home. Provide examples from Briana's life of school-initiated communication and home-initiated teaming.

**Family Support: Briana's Family**

11. We are fortunate to meet several of Briana's extended family members, including her older brother, grandmother, aunt, and cousin. What are some of the important contributions that extended family members make to the growth of an exceptional young person like Briana?

**Family Support: Briana's Family**

12. In what ways is Briana's growth promoted by living in a family where there is solid support but also high expectations to contribute meaningfully to and get along with the family?

**Community & Contributions: Collaboration**

13. A familiar challenge for Briana's support team is making decisions about when to place her among peers in her middle school versus placing her with more advanced classmates, i.e., the high school science and math courses. What are the critical issues that her team must confront while making these important decisions?

**Community & Contributions: Collaboration**
14. What case can be made for expecting and anticipating that Briana's peers, those her age and those older, will provide important supports for her ongoing growth and development in addition to the services provided by professionals and family?

**Community & Contributions: Extracurricular**
15. In what ways has Briana enriched and contributed to the lives of all those she associates with, including school, family, and community circles?

**Community & Contributions: Extracurricular**
16. In what ways can you perceive building on Briana's strengths, e.g., her singing, dancing, and church service, to involve her with the larger school and neighborhood community?

**Community & Contributions: Vision & Advice**
17. Why is it so important for members of Briana's support team to envision her future including the special vision her mother has for her that Briana be "a balanced person"?

**Community & Contributions: Vision & Advice**
18. What are some key thoughts, attitudes, and actions you might emulate in your work with exceptional children based on advice from members of Briana's support team?

**Beyond School**
**Work Place: Jael, Age 20**
1. Will Jael be able to be a paraeducator once she graduates? What skills is she learning at TRACE that allow her to be a teaching assistant?

**Work Place: Jael, Age 20**
2. What insights did Jael show toward students with problem behaviors? Were you surprised at her advice? Why or why not?

**Work Place: Rachel, Age 26**
3. How important is it for individuals with disabilities to follow their dreams? How much of Rachel's success is due to her really wanting to work as a secretary?

**Work Place: Rachel, Age 26**
4. Rachel is able to complete most of her job independently, but she will still receive 20% intervention assistance from her job coach for the next few months. Will Rachel continue to be successful once Beth is no longer working with her? Why or why not?

**Work Place: Maxine, Age 50**
5. What did you think of the reactions from the two students?

**Work Place: Maxine, Age 50**
6. Do you also find her story as inspirational as they did? Why or why not?

**Exploring Talents: Karen, Facilitator**

7. What benefits would students with disabilities receive by working on service learning projects like Project Success and interacting outside school with students who do not have disabilities?

**Exploring Talents: Karen, Facilitator**

8. What benefits would students with no disabilities receive by working on service learning projects like Project Success and interacting outside school with students who do have disabilities?

**Exploring Talents: Jamie, Age 20**

9. Jamie was the first person to volunteer an idea in the group discussion shown on the video. What does that say about how she feels participating with her peers in this setting?

**Exploring Talents: Jamie, Age 20**

10. What does Jamie learn from participating in a group that is helping to get books for children in need?

**Exploring Talents: Jonathan, Age 18**

11. How was Jonathan included in the Project Success project? What activities did he participate in?

**Exploring Talents: Jonathan, Age 18**

12. Were there other ways in which Jonathan could have participated in the project?

**Pursuing Interests: Kristen, Age 33**

13. Kristen has multiple disabilities (blindness, language disorder). Have her talents helped her to overcome the limitations of her disabilities? How?

**Pursuing Interests: Kristen, Age 33**

14. Do all people have hidden talents? Do you believe finding such talents opens the door to additional opportunities in the community?

**Pursuing Interests: Greg, Age 39**

15. Greg discussed having to sell himself to get the job he wanted and the services he needed. Do you believe people skills can be taught to individuals with disabilities?

**Pursuing Interests: Greg, Age 39**

16. Greg is also involved with People First, an advocacy group for individuals with disabilities. How important is it for Greg or other individuals with disabilities to participate in advocacy groups?

**Pursuing Interests: MeMe, Age 51**

17. Both MeMe and Greg mentioned how important public transportation is for them to be able to function in the community. After seeing how long it takes MeMe to get on the bus, how much more time and effort do you believe it takes a person with disabilities to get around than a person without disabilities?

**Pursuing Interests: MeMe, Age 51**

18. MeMe and Greg are a couple. Do you believe social relationships between individuals with disabilities are the same or different than relationships between individuals without disabilities? Give examples of why you believe they would be the same or different.

## Answer Key to Practice Quizzes

| # | Ch. 1 | Ch. 2 | Ch. 3 | Ch. 4 | Ch. 5 | Ch. 6 | Ch. 7 | Ch. 8 | Ch. 9 | Ch. 10 | Ch. 11 | Ch. 12 | Ch. 13 | Ch. 14 | Ch. 15 | Ch. 16 |
|---|---|---|---|---|---|---|---|---|---|---|---|---|---|---|---|---|
| 1 | A | C | B | A | B | B | B | B | A | A | C | A | B | D | B | C |
| 2 | D | A | A | C | C | C | D | A | B | C | D | C | C | B | B | C |
| 3 | B | B | A | B | B | D | B | B | C | B | C | A | A | A | D | A |
| 4 | B | B | A | D | B | A | C | A | B | C | A | C | B | B | B | D |
| 5 | A | C | D | C | C | D | A | C | C | A | C | A | D | B | A | C |
| 6 | B | C | D | C | C | B | D | C | C | A | C | B | B | C | D | A |
| 7 | B | C | B | C | B | C | C | C | D | C | C | B | A | A | B | C |
| 8 | C | B | D | A | D | C | C | B | C | A | A | A | D | D | A | D |
| 9 | D | C | D | B | B | A | B | D | C | B | C | C | A | A | C | D |
| 10 | B | B | B | A | D | D | C | D | D | D | C | B | C | B | B | D |
| 11 | C | B | A | A | D | C | B | B | B | B | C | C | D | C | C | C |
| 12 | A | D | B | D | D | A | B | B | A | A | B | D | B | B | C | D |
| 13 | A | A | A | D | B | B | A | D | A | C | C | B | B | C | D | B |
| 14 | D | D | C | A | D | B | a | A | C | A | C | B | D | C | D | B |
| 15 | C | D | B | D | B | C | C | A | A | D | B | C | D | A | C | C |